First published: 2011
© Copyright Colin Palfrey & Y Lolfa Cyf., 2011

ISBN: 978 - 1- 84771 - 372 - 8

Cartoons: Elwyn Ioan & Siôn Jones
Cover cartoon: Siôn Jones
Design: Y Lolfa

Published and printed in Wales
on paper from well managed forests
by Y Lolfa Cyf., Talybont, Ceredigion SY24 5HE
website www.ylolfa.com
email ylolfa@ylolfa.com
tel 01970 832 304
fax 01970 832 304

Wacky Wales

A guide to Wales by Colin Palfrey

y Lolfa

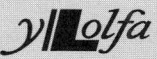

Introduction

'CROESO I GYMRU' – 'Welcome to Wales'. Yes, welcome to the Land of Song. That's a bold claim but it's certainly the land of singers. Think of Sir Geraint Evans and Dame Margaret Price. Then there's Bryn Terfel and Katherine Jenkins. Sir – yes, Sir Tom Jones and Dame Shirley Bassey and latterly Cerys Matthews, Charlotte Church and bands such as the Manic Street Preachers, The Stereophonics and Super Furry Animals. I could go on but let us not be too boastful. Let's just say that per head of population Wales is the most talented nation in the world. This small country of around 3 million people has produced famous politicians, sporting superstars and eminent writers and actors.

Probably the only challengers to this assertion are the Italians. Da Vinci, Michelangelo, Botticelli, Verdi, Puccini, Gigli and Pavarotti spring to mind. Don't mention Mussolini; he couldn't paint or compose or even sing though he was quite good at shouting. They've got a few decent footballers and their rugby squad is improving with every season. But we're much better than them at playing the harp and clog dancing. Anyway, they must feel an affinity with Wales and the Welsh because in some valley towns there are probably as many Servinis, Contis and Riccis as there are Davieses. (Come to think of it, they probably cook better than us as well.)

But apart from a male voice choir in every village, what else can Wales offer you as a would-be visitor? Wherever you stay in Wales the mountains are never far away, beckoning. Only a pony trek away from the once most industrialised town in Europe (Merthyr) the Brecon Beacons beckon. But beware – the area can be dangerous; far more than one experienced climber has been found among the mist-swirled ledges, in a horizontal position, his packed lunch only half-eaten.

But Wales can offer the discriminating tourist more than just awesome scenery: mountains, lakes, green valleys and miles of exquisite caravan parks. It can offer the excitement of communal cockle-gathering, underground pony-trekking in disused coal mines and the sheer exhilaration of water-skiing on the back of a donkey at one of the country's many seaside resorts. And don't be put off by foul rumours about the weather. We do get a lot of rain in Wales but we also get lots of snow, sleet, hailstorms, tornados and hurricanes. 'Just pack an anorak' is the Wales Tourist Board's slick slogan. So here is a guide to what you can expect to enjoy in your visit to this little gem.

COLIN PALFREY

Events

The National Eisteddfod

This festival of the arts attracts many thousands of visitors every year. It is the one major event in which everything is conducted through the medium of the Welsh language, except for the sculptures which tend to be mute and sometimes English. One of the main competitions is open to all visitors and takes place in the big tent or pavilion. This is (in translation) the Audience Endurance Medal which is awarded to the member of the public who can remain in her or his seat (visits to the *tŷ bach* (loo) permitted, through a minimum of ten renderings of the same folk song, five clog dances, twenty

Another competition (in the Eisteddfod) is the Fancy Dress. This lot came last.

four choral recitations and at least thirty-five individual adjudications. The record for this stamina-sapping test is held by a farmer from Ceredigion whose hobby is listed in the Eisteddfod's 'Who's Who' as counting three-legged sheep.

The climax of the week is the Chairing of the Bard. In the past this prize has been withheld because the actual chair was not considered to be of a sufficiently high standard. (One – like the farmer's sheep – had only three legs.) Nowadays, the highly complicated construction of traditional Welsh verse forms on which the major prizes are based are worked out on computers, so in theory anyone can enter. Indeed, the last two winners of the formal verse competitions have been a Persian cat from Blaenau Ffestiniog who apparently casually walked over the computer keyboard when his owner was out of the room and 'A Welsh-speaking budgie from Rhyl' – the words in quotes being a translation of the opening line of the winning poem produced by the feathered bard.

Perhaps the most emotional part of the whole festival is the day when visitors from overseas are given a tumultuous croeso (welcome). This

moment belongs to all those Welsh exiles who decided long ago to settle abroad and make a few dollars – they are mainly from the USA – but who remain loyal on one day a year to their homeland. There is a special tent set aside for them staffed by medical personnel. So, if you catch sight of a long line of senior citizens, some of them in funny hats and, for couples, matching Hawaiian shirts you will probably be witnessing the Inoculation ceremony. In a secret location somewhere in north Wales a pure Welsh culture has been preserved by members of the *Gorsedd* (see picture p.6). A minute quantity of this culture is injected into the visitors from other lands in order to top up their Welshness for another twelve months. A precise dose of the culture must be administered; too little and they may never return; too much and they may be tempted to sell up and buy Anglesey.

The Urdd Eisteddfod is exclusively for younger contestants, a key feature of which is the children's choral singing competition. Here you

Spaceships landing at the 1994 Eisteddfod

can see earnest teachers coaxing the maximum performance out of well-drilled pupils all singing in tune and bending their heads forward at the statutory dip of fifteen degrees. The choir which can go the longest time without laughing at their conductor's facial contortions is declared the winner. There is a complex scale of points that are subtracted from the maximum of twenty.

For example, two points are taken off for a titter, five for a fairly obvious and outright giggle, ten for a guffaw and if any chorister is seen rolling on the floor in uncontrollable laughter the whole choir is automatically disqualified.

The International Eisteddfod

This annual event tales place in a beautiful part of Wales just outside the village or small town of Llangollen. Choirs, dancers and musicians travel from many parts of the world to compete against each other and in the evenings there are concerts by professional performers. The abundance of flowers on the stage might lead you to believe you are in a horticultural show rather than an eisteddfod but this does not detract from the colour of various national costumes. What, you might ask, is the Welsh national costume? For men there is a growing market for tartan kilts and other articles of wear. The McDavies and McEvans clans are good sellers. As for the ladies, the neat puritanical outfits worn during the *Dawns y Werin* (Country Dancing) is as near as you can get to a national dress forgetting, of course, the steeple-like hats featured in paintings of old ladies in chapel. We shall discover later in the book who invented this bit of millinery, although with a slightly more pointed tip they would be in danger of

9

transforming a Bible-reading granny into a witch.

The Royal Welsh Show

Llanelwedd, near Builth Wells, is the venue for this annual celebration of things rural. The admission fee might mean you will have to forego lunch but try to arrive early in the day otherwise all you are likely to see are the faces or backs of other visitors. In the various arenas traditional farming arts, crafts and pleasures abound. Over here the sheep-shearing competition using only a pair of nail scissors (This competition usually goes on well into the evening), over there the 'Guess the weight of the bull by lying under it' contest (This competition often doesn't actually get started). The show, of course, has royal patronage so a visit from one of the Royal Family usually happens during the week. It is often difficult to spot the royals as they dress up as farmers and all farmers and farmers' wives look the same.

Flora and Fauna

For the nature lover there can be few more exciting places to spend a holiday than Wales. Here, in a small land, are numerous varieties of animal life not seen anywhere else in the world – species left undiscovered by Darwin and prehistorians, genetic throwbacks to a more primeval era in Welsh history.

One impressive example is Neanderthal Dai. This is a form of anthropoid-cum-human who emerges from undiscovered valleys locations during the rugby international Six Nations series. They are instantly recognisable by their unusual shape resembling huge red-clad ostrich eggs with short fat legs and arms. They communicate with each other mainly in coarse grunts. These are thirsty creatures who can drink continuously for twelve hours. Their natural diet is meat pies and chips as they have adapted to the urban environments rather like the Cardiff pigeon. On good authority it has been established that Cardiff – the capital of Wales – has the largest population of pigeons in the UK. At outdoor cafes you will see a family of these intelligent birds sitting around a table. If you're lucky they may toss you a few crumbs of a left-over sandwich; if you're unlucky you might come away with white shoulders. These fascinating birds have become the obsession of grown men who meet in secret in the twilight zone of the major Welsh towns. Among the gay bars and Masonic halls you might notice a workmen's club or a disused church hall where within meets a circle of pigeon fanciers. 'Circle' is not the collective noun for a group of pigeon fanciers. This is 'a herd' or 'a nerd'...

This pastime has an odd history, for the word 'fancy' appears now to have completely altered its meaning over the years. Now these ardent enemies of the humble pigeon go to great lengths to capture the birds, take them in trucks and cars to remote spots and let them go, presumably to reduce the numbers perching around city buildings. Unfortunately, most of these birds fly back to their luckless captors only to have the same treatment inflicted on them week after week. Apparently, any suggestion that it would be more humane to shoot the pigeons is strongly resisted by the 'fanciers'.

Other animals form the centrepiece of Welsh sports and shows. One of these is a lurcher – a cross between a border collie and a rug. This dog, with its ally the terrier, forms a deadly duo that has been known to flush from their holes rabbits, badgers, foxes and, in times past, the occasional miner. The Welsh corgi, so beloved by the Royal family, is an aggressive little dog that bites the ankles of cattle. They are known as the Welsh scrum halves of the animal kingdom.

Among the sheep of Wales one breed stands out – the south Wales valley sheep, known officially as 'dafad acrobaticus'. Most farms of any size in south Wales have a gymnasium attached where, from an early age, the sheep are trained in the art of commando-style manoeuvres. In order to eke out their meagre EU subsidies, the farmers in this part of Wales have to make sure their sheep gain access to every blade of grass available – from churchyards to back gardens. Walls, cattle grids and fences are no barrier to these engaging creatures. If

they can't get over them they usually eat their way through them. Indeed, scientific tests have discovered in the intestines of dead valleys sheep a whole range of objects such as leaves, wire wool, underpants and the complete works of R. S. Thomas (paperback edition).

Animals also play a central part in Welsh legends – is there really a monster in Bala Lake (*Llyn Tegid*)? Did dragons ever roam the mountains of Wales? Is it true that the ratio of dogs per council house is 3.5 to 1? But for the true symbols of Wales we turn to the humble leek and daffodil, which taste roughly the same. While there are few competitions to grow the biggest daffodil, local horticultural shows feature gigantic leeks, some as thick as a goalpost and tasting roughly the same. While these are easily recognisable, the lonely whinberry growing wild on moor and mountain can sometimes be mistaken for other less succulent offerings. Many a tourist, having spent ten hours halfway up a Welsh mountain intent on picking whinberries or bilberries, has gone back to his self-catering chalet only to squander a vintage Burgundy on a pie whose main ingredient turned out to be sheep's droppings.

Sport and recreation

Wales is not an aggressive nation. While some national anthems pay tribute to military heroes and exclaim the hope that they will expand and conquer, the Welsh national anthem extols its poets and singers and its hope is that the Welsh language will flourish. So all the testosterone is channelled into rugby. Wales now proudly hosts international matches at the grand Millennium Stadium next door to the famous Cardiff Arms Park. Wealthy people can buy debentures – which means that they are guaranteed tickets to watch every home match – a privilege that is of doubtful value during one of the Welsh team's many off seasons. In

Wales rugby is said to be more of a religion than a sport and until very recently there was a dwindling bunch of believers. At least you don't have to pay half your week's wages to get into a church or chapel – or synagogue or mosque for that matter.

For those visitors to Wales who prefer to take part rather than just watch there are countless opportunities in sporting Wales. Why not try water-skiing on the moat around Caerphilly Castle? You're sure to attract an appreciative crowd including one or two council officials. Or why not book in for some hang-gliding sessions in Cardiff? Jump off the top of the Pearl Building in Cardiff and let the warm air currents blowing from the capital city's numerous Bangladeshi restaurants waft you where they will. Don't worry if you are carried further than you intended. Each hang-gliding participant is ringed by volunteers from the local pigeon fanciers club so wherever you may land, the hired equipment can be returned to the Council in the stamped addressed twelve metre square box that each hang-glider carries on his/her back.

In the north, for the really adventurous, there is the challenge of Welsh rock climbing. Giant sticks of rock bearing the message 'Llandudno lives' are thrust deep into the sand. Standing on the top of the rock on a clear day you can see the tip of 'Little England beyond Wales'. This is called Newport.

Entertainment

From casinos to clog dancing, telly to twmpath, Wales has it all. Choirs, harpists, folk singers are ready to entertain you at the drop of a Welsh hat. Music and arts centres are springing up in all corners of Wales and these cater for all tastes – from chamber music and poetry readings to lectures on wool dyeing and exhibitions of contemporary toothpicks.

At the more avant-garde centres in the major towns and cities you can listen to a free lunchtime recital of early Bolivian love songs played on authentic flower pots or watch forgotten masterpieces of the cinema such as the Swedish 'Tribute to Spring', a three hour epic which

portrays a marigold growing in slow motion. The *Cymanfa Ganu* is still a vibrant event in the chapel calendar. No such gala of singing is complete without *Hwyl* – he is the conductor who will tell you when to stand up and sit down, when to sing loud or soft or when to whip round with the collection box. Everyone in the village attends the *Cymanfa;* if you don't they might be singing about you.

Bingo is very popular in many parts of Wales. But don't expect a riotous or even a mildly amusing evening. Participants must observe a solemn silence during the 'calling of the numbers'. All politically incorrect references to two fat ladies (88) have now been eradicated. The number 88 is now preceded by the high priest's (*Bingo caller's*) exclamation, 'Two morbidly obese females'. Anybody interrupting the high priest during his intoning of the mystic numbers – it's almost always a male – will be excommunicated on the spot unless they are in a state of near spiritual ecstasy when they are permitted to shout out 'Hallelujah! (*'House!'*).

Sometimes prisons are used as bingo halls.

Eating and drinking

Mention Wales and you immediately think of laver bread and cockles. Many visitors to Wales shy away from laver bread because it looks rather like the third layer of a

15

compost heap. At one time this Welsh delicacy was thought to have been processed from seaweed; nowadays it is more widely known that it is actually made from washing up cloths impregnated with Guinness. Buy it from the local market where the friendly stall-holders will tell you what to do with it. If you're used to eating moss and sand with your bacon then laver bread is for you.

Chitterlings are another traditional Welsh delicacy and are often eaten ungarnished. They are the smaller intestines of a pig or other edible animals. Since virtually all animals are edible they might be from a badger or pine marten. In former days a necklace of chitterlings was said to keep diseases away as well as most other people. *Cawl cennin* (leek soup) and lamb cooked in honey feature in the Welsh banquets now so popular throughout Wales. For those with less adventurous palates why not try the Welsh burger – compressed chitterlings and laver bread served up in a bap. Penclawdd cockles are another renowned Welsh dish. Some of these shellfish are so large that after you've

eaten the inside you can use the shell as a boat to catch more cockles. It then becomes known as a coracle. What better to clean out the colon than to have a plateful of cockles and laver bread with a Caerphilly cheese Welsh rarebit washed down with a pint of good honest Welsh ale?

And there are now several breweries across all parts of Wales. While the beers they produce are gaining widespread popularity, the local wines have a distinctive bouquet and taste that must be acquired. There are one or two vineyards in

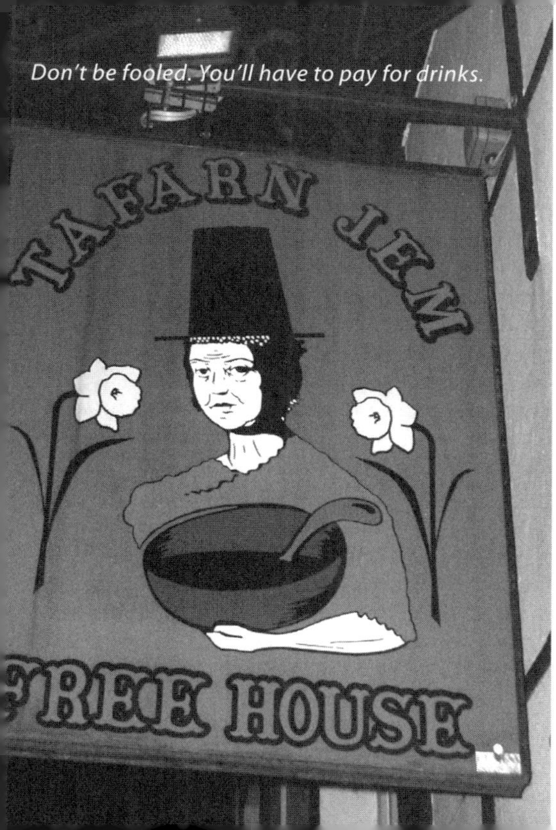
TAFARN JEM
FREE HOUSE
Don't be fooled. You'll have to pay for drinks.

Wales and since the weather here varies from wet to very wet the growing season is short. So the cunning Welsh entrepreneurs use peas instead. There is not a more traditionally Welsh sight than a bevy of *y werin* (ordinary folk) up to

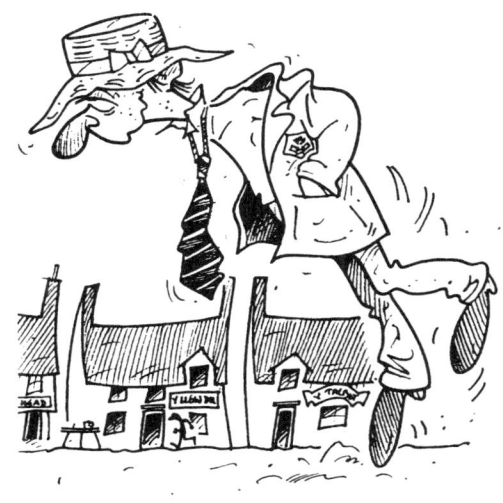

their ankles in peas, treading the pods to make instant pea wine. Some uncharitable locals drop the word 'wine' when referring to this drink. Many a welsh maiden aunt who would never dream of entering a pub will be happy enough to regale you, the visitor, with her home-made wine. After a glass or two you won't want to leave. After a few more you won't be able to! You might also like to enter the local beer swilling competitions. These are usually held in rugby clubs where, for a nominal fee, you can be signed in by a member. The regulars welcome a sporting challenge but make sure that if you do enter as a competitor you don't actually win – especially if you're English.

Here's our Mam at the minibar.

Buildings

Of course, you cannot come to Wales without visiting some of its historic monuments. Most impressive of these are the castles, from the colossal splendour of Caernarfon castle to the tiny folly of Castell Coch near Cardiff, or the extravaganza of Portmeirion inspired by a dream after the architect – Clough Williams-Ellis – had been dining on smoked mackerel, pâté de fois gras and a tin of curried beans.

There are also some outstanding religious buildings in Wales. Carved into the rock at *San Gofan* (St Govan's), not far from Pembroke is probably the smallest chapel in Wales or even the UK. In earlier times smugglers and puffins formed the major part of the congregation. Today it remains a sanctuary for the more hardy courting couples. The cathedrals of St David's and Llandaff and the noble ruins at Llanthony,

Tintern and Lamphey Palace contrast in their splendour with the neat symmetry of the typical Welsh chapel

Some of the most interesting buildings of their type found throughout Wales – such as chapels, woollen mills, shops and pigsties – have been removed and reconstructed at St Fagan's Museum of Welsh Life near Cardiff. Most of the staff who stand in the buildings also look as if they were removed and reconstructed from an earlier era. For a more futuristic building, visit the National Botanic Garden near Carmarthen. It proves that Wales is not just about coal mines and coracles. The Millennium Centre in the Bay (erstwhile 'docks') in Cardiff is another impressive structure that has been likened to an armadillo. It would have been even

An example of really quality graffiti

more impressive if it had been blessed with a few exotic or even run-of-the-mill vegetation. As it is, the much-vaunted reconstruction of the docks looks as if the designers had an aversion to the colour green. Welsh slate and acres of glass in the Millennium Centre and Welsh Assembly HQ need the odd touch of tree or bush to relieve the stark, once maritime landscape.

Where to stay

Wales offers the full range of tourist accommodation – from modest guest-houses to plush hostelries. For those who want the luxury of a five-star hotel but want to pay a little less than the normal tariff, why not rent an apartment in one of the recently built Council offices that adorn some of the most depressed areas of Wales? In the holiday season you can stay in the Chief Executive's suite with its self-

contained bathroom facilities and well-equipped cocktail cabinet. The administrative staff will be pleased to arrange his or her schedule of meetings to fit in with your holiday plans so the CE will only need to pop in occasionally to check e-mails and to empty the in-tray (most CEs nowadays are house-trained). Nobody in Wales will moan about paying excessive Council Tax if they know that these sumptuous multi-million pound offices are attracting tourists.

At the other end of the scale is the seaside guest-house.

Make sure you read the rules of the house carefully. Breakfast, for example, is normally served at a time when you would not usually be up for work, let alone on holiday. Facing a plate of tinned tomatoes floating on bacon fat might not be everyone's idea of a good start to the day, and since the breakfast menu remains the same all week, those with a delicate constitution may prefer to have a lie-in until 9 a.m. when the knock on the door heralds the arrival of bed-making time. In the better guest-houses the landlady might even do this for you.

Guests are often allowed to stay out as late as 9 p.m. on weekdays, with a half hour extension on Saturdays for good behaviour. Guest-houses are not licensed for alcoholic drinks, and in the more temperate zones you might have to take a breath test before being allowed in.

A politically incorrect watering hole

Useful tips

The following suggestions should help you to get the most out of your visit to Wales:

1. Do not be offended if you should hear the Welsh language being spoken in shops, pubs and other places of interest. Although in times past there were moves to make conversing in the national tongue an offence other than between consenting adults in private, it is now acceptable for all persons who speak Welsh to do so. If you think that they are talking about you, there are psychiatrists on hand who are experts in treating paranoia. However, if you are sensitive about French people speaking French or Spaniards talking in Spanish when you visit their countries, try easing yourself out of this condition by listening to the denizens of Birmingham or Liverpool conversing in their own distinctive version of English.

2. If you are travelling by road be patient, especially if you are motoring via Builth Wells, Llandrindod Wells or Rhayader. Roads in this area of Wales were built by the Romans for their chariot Grand Prix – hence the number of sharp bends. In the peak holiday season traffic moves so slowly you should be able to pick blackberries as you drive along.

3. Be prepared for the weather. Wales is a mountainous country and there is a good deal of rain. If you are staying in a guest-house or rural hotel, look for the tell-tale signs of moss on the carpet and toadstools on the walls before you pay the deposit. Sou'westers and wellies are recommended beach-wear and may be hired along with deck chairs and reinforced steel wind-breaks.

4. Visitors should appreciate that there is a strong nonconformist tradition in Wales. Consequently there are very few naturist beaches. Nude bathing is only permitted for the

under-fives. Grown females may only appear topless with the special permission of the local leisure and amenities committee. Please enclose a recent photograph and a completed application form, which can be obtained from the deck-chair attendant.

5. Not everyone wishes to spend their holiday money on alcohol unless you get caught up in a rugby international weekend. Fortunately in Wales there are a number of temperance hotels and guest-houses frequented by elderly spinsters and ex-Felinfoel drinkers. Different social activities are organised every weekday evening and range from silent beetle drives to the famous yard of Ovaltine drinking contest.

6. Local customs apply in some of the interesting markets which are to be found in all corners of Wales. In the Cardigan area, for example, stall-holders barter with the customers to increase the asking price. Using one of the many excellent Basic Guides to Welsh such as Welsh for Dummies and Welsh for Brummies, why not learn something of the language and try it out at the local market. Some errors may creep in and the occasional visitor has had to hire a trailer to take home the odd sheep or two after mistakenly believing they had bought a bag of laver bread, but the results are usually well worth the effort.

6. Over the page are some useful words and phrases:

- Tŷ bach – *Toilet*
- A oes meddyg yn y tŷ? – *Is there a doctor in the house?*
- A oes meddyg yn y tŷ bach? – *Is there a doctor in the toilet?*
- Saith, deg ac un deg saith – *Chicken chop suey, curried octopus and prawn crackers*
- Ble mae fy nhrowsus? – *That was quite a party!*
- Symud dy din. – *Excuse me but you appear to be sitting on my towel.*
- Mae'r cwrw yma'n rhy wan! – *There's beer in my water!*
- A oes heddwch? – *Can you keep the noise down please.*
- Canolfan siopa – *Mental hospital*
- Gorsedd y Beirdd – *Transvestites*
- Ble mae'r gwaith carthffosiaeth? – *Where's the beach?*
- Llwybr cyhoeddus – *Public footpath*
- Llwybr Preifat – *Beware of the bull*
- Oes gennych chi ganiatad cynllunio? – *No sandcastles allowed.*
- Rwyf eisiau llyfu pen-ôl y frenhines. – *I would like a first class stamp.*
- Mae'r mul yma'n uniaith Gymraeg. – *This donkey is deaf.*
- Rwyf yn sgrechian – *Ice cream*
- Dim ysmygu – *Keep off the grass*
- Creigiau Preseli – *Elvis rocks*
- Carchar – *Holiday camp*
- Iechyd da! – *Cancel the ambulance.*
- Ble mae'r archfarchnad? – *I'm off my trolley!*

WHERE TO GO

Abergele

The town is halfway between Rhyl and Colwyn Bay on what is called the North Wales Riviera but is actually a mile from the sea. A mile to the west of the town is Gwrych Castle, a mock antique building described by some as 'spooky'. Surely all castles are spooky, especially if you book a room overnight and it turns out to be the dungeon where there's only cold running water – down the walls. In 1868 there was a rail disaster here involving the mail train from Euston to Holyhead. There were probably leaves on the line.

Bala

A demure town bordering the largest and probably deepest natural lake in Wales. Hidden beneath the depths is not a fabulous monster but a shy fish called a *gwyniad* [coregonus pennantii] which is unique to this stretch of water. But how did it get there in the first place? And is it a protected species? If caught, does it have to be presented to the Queen? And has it ever – perhaps unknowingly – been eaten with chips? Mysteries such as this abound in parts of north Wales and add piquancy to the inquisitive tourist's adventures.

Here lived Thomas Charles who founded the British and Foreign Bible Society after giving his own Bible to Mary Jones, a young girl who had walked barefoot several miles to visit him. It was a good job he was in. Statues are often susceptible to being adorned with cones for the head and beer cans for the outstretched hand, and the one dedicated to T. I. Ellis MP is no exception. In 1886 he became the first Liberal MP for Meirionnydd, beating famous Irish politician Charles Parnell for the nomination. But what was an Irish leader doing on the Welsh political scene? Another mystery.

A packed pub in Bangor

Bangor

This is a cathedral town situated at the entrance to the Menai Straits. Students occupy upper Bangor which is quite cosmopolitan – local greengrocers sell guavas, mangoes and lychees. Some local people have never seen a guava and most think that a lychee is something local GPs use to suck blood from their patients. Bangor has a pier, even though it can hardly be classed a resort – except perhaps as a last resort.

Here stood one of the earliest monasteries in Britain until the Saxons came to the area putting many monks to the sword whilst the rest fled across the sea to Bardsey Island (*Ynys Enlli*). What prompted this onslaught was possibly the tatty souvenirs sold to the Saxons by the ever worldly holy brothers. Some monks, of course, sell monastery-made alcoholic drinks. The strength of some of the drinks is formidable and might account for the founding of Trappist settlements. Try talking after a firkin of 14% real ale! (See also *Tenby,* where you will find a similar hazard presented by the monks who inhabit Caldey Island.)

Barmouth (Y Bermo)

Possibly the only town this side of the Andes to be built in a vertical fashion. Barmouth stands on the estuary of the Mawddach river and has glorious views of the Cader Idris mountain range. Picturesque perhaps, the town is not noted for its fine architecture or ancient

then running 72 miles. This challenge makes the triathlon look like a day out for wimps. In the human versus animal event mountain goats usually polish off the Three Peaks in no time at all and are on a par with humans on the running bit but they offer very little competition during the sailing phase.

Beaumaris

The very name of this impressive fortified town bears witness to the Norman incursions throughout Wales. Here also Edward I built a concentric castle in 1295 in his attempt to hold the Welsh in check. Strange how Roman, Norman and Teutonic invaders have found attacking Welsh people such an irresistible pastime over the centuries. But we must take these historic and many current efforts to put the Welsh down as born of envy and some resentment; envy perhaps of our stunning scenery and the prodigious talent and resentment, perhaps, that despite intermittent colonisation and globalisation the Welsh

monuments apart from the blue-rinsed variety who huddle together on the promenade. The town boasts numerous amusement arcades which gives some indication of its cultural profile. But there are less sedentary amusements on offer. Here is the start of the Three Peaks race which involves sailing to Scotland, climbing the highest mountain in Wales (Snowdon), England (Scafell Pike) and Scotland (Ben Nevis) and

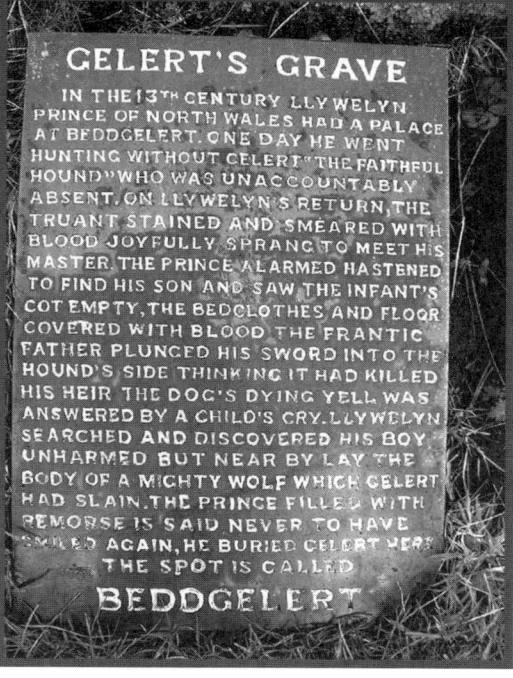

GELERT'S GRAVE

IN THE 13TH CENTURY LLYWELYN PRINCE OF NORTH WALES HAD A PALACE AT BEDDGELERT. ONE DAY HE WENT HUNTING WITHOUT GELERT "THE FAITHFUL HOUND" WHO WAS UNACCOUNTABLY ABSENT. ON LLYWELYN'S RETURN, THE TRUANT STAINED AND SMEARED WITH BLOOD JOYFULLY SPRANG TO MEET HIS MASTER. THE PRINCE ALARMED HASTENED TO FIND HIS SON AND SAW THE INFANT'S COT EMPTY, THE BEDCLOTHES, AND FLOOR COVERED WITH BLOOD THE FRANTIC FATHER PLUNGED HIS SWORD INTO THE HOUND'S SIDE THINKING IT HAD KILLED HIS HEIR THE DOG'S DYING YELL WAS ANSWERED BY A CHILD'S CRY. LLYWELYN SEARCHED AND DISCOVERED HIS BOY UNHARMED BUT NEAR BY LAY THE BODY OF A MIGHTY WOLF WHICH GELERT HAD SLAIN. THE PRINCE FILLED WITH REMORSE IS SAID NEVER TO HAVE SMILED AGAIN. HE BURIED GELERT HERE THE SPOT IS CALLED

BEDDGELERT

language is alive and kicking.

Now we welcome invaders of a more gentle nature; tourists – not merely for their money but because indigenous Welsh people are friendly – perhaps at times over-friendly – by nature.

Beddgelert

Nowhere but in Wales could a village have attained notoriety through a dog's grave. This is Beddgelert's one claim to fame. The name means 'Gelert's grave'. That sounds impressive. Beddfido just doesn't have the same ring about it. Gelert was no ordinary hound. He was Prince Llewelyn's best friend, which might tell us something about his (the Prince's) social life. Left in charge of the royal offspring one day, Gelert saved the child from a marauding wolf. On his return, Llewelyn mistook the blood and gore for that of the junior prince's remains and put poor Gelert to the sword. It was not long after this unfortunate incident that the RSPCA was founded.

If you shed a tear at the grave of this seriously

misunderstood dog make sure you are standing in the right place since there are many headstones standing in the field. Iron railings surround the supposed headstone of Gelert. Nowadays, doting dog lovers would probably have had Gelert stuffed for posterity. And why not? We do the same to turkeys and chickens.

Bethesda

The small settlement nestles in the Ogwen valley amidst some of the

highest mountains in Wales. Carnedd Llywelyn and Carnedd Dafydd (numbers 2 and 3 in heig to Snowdon itself) are a stone's throw away – c should that be a slate's throw away. There are certainly enough of them around to throw.

Bethesda was home to the famous Penrhyn slate quarry and examples of its multi-coloured product can be found the world over. Bethesda

On the way to market, sheep get a comfortable ride

is a Hebrew word meaning 'healing pool' but in Wales it is the name of countless nonconformist chapels. Their congregations are often described as dry. This could be a symptom of slate dust.

Betws-y-coed

If you're heading towards Snowdonia from the Midlands, as thousands do – there's only one way to go and that's through Betws-y-coed. During high summer – that's the day in the year when it's not raining – the tortuous bends and narrow roads are packed with nose-to-tail cars and coaches. Many have suggested that this village is the prime reason for so many English people settling in north Wales – they just can't face going through it all again on the way back.

Local attractions include the Fairy Glen – also known as the fay butcher and the spectacular Swallow Falls (*Rhaeadr Ewynnol*). Many tourists queue up and pay to see the waterfalls – not content with viewing Welsh water in captivity (bath night). Nowadays entrepreneurs bottle water and sell it at ludicrous prices to customers who seem to have been convinced that all tap water needs to be boiled before it's consumed. Who knows how many anti-social cattle or sheep have relieved themselves as they lap up the running water. Nuff said.

Blaenau Ffestiniog

Set high in the horseshoe created by the Moelwyn and Manod mountains, BF is synonymous with slate. Everything here is made of slate – houses, roofs, fences, paving stones, windows (it's always raining here so non-one wants to see out). All that remains of the working ways of the quarrymen can be found in the town's main tourist attractions – the Gloddfa Ganol Slate Mine and the Llechwedd Slate Caverns.

If you don't relish going underground, hop onto the narrow gauge railway. Built originally to ferry slates to Porthmadog for export, it now imports tourists.

Caernarfon

Not since 1282 has there been a Prince of Wales. However, in 1969 a re-creation was staged in the castle by a long-forgotten Hollywood producer and the spectacle gained a worldwide audience. As the bards processed into the castle an American was heard to say: 'Hey – who are those guys wearing shrouds?' The leading actor and supporting cast have rarely been seen since.

The phenomenon that amazes visitors is that almost everybody speaks Welsh and no matter how ugly you are, shop assistants will automatically greet you as *'Del'* – an informal term of endearment meaning handsome or pretty; or even address you as *'cyw'* meaning 'chick' (regardless of your sex – or lack of it). The Welsh spoken by the natives – the ones with bones through their noses – is a rather guttural dialect using Welsh words unfamiliar to their Welsh-speaking compatriots further south. These tribes are known as 'gogs' because they live in the 'gogledd' (north) of Wales. It was the north Wales accent that Shakespeare latched

A Caernarfon restaurant.

onto in his depiction of Welsh characters. North Walians can't pronounce the 'z' sound so if you are told that someone has 'sauce' all over their face it's not that they've been careless with the ketchup; the likelihood is that they're suffering from acne.

Conwy

Conwy enjoys the reputation of being one of Wales's premier tourist attractions – mainly due to Edward I's castle (yes – him again). In contrast to this large structure is the smallest house in Britain. This was occupied from the 1500s until 1900, the last occupant being a six foot fisherman. He enjoyed living there despite the cramped conditions because he could dust the bedroom ceiling while boiling his breakfast egg. In anyone's language (apart from estate agents') this house is tiny. In their language it is 'unusually bijou'.

For bridge enthusiasts (not the North–South shin-kicking variety but the architectural version) there is the tubular railway bridge devised by Robert Stephenson and the suspension bridge created by Thomas Telford in 1826.

Corwen

The Owain Glyndŵr Hotel in the centre of this small market town bears testimony to Corwen's connection with the famous Welsh rebel. Perhaps he popped down to Cardiff as well because there is a pub by the same name there. An old legend claims

that a cross engraved on a stone lintel above the door of the local church was caused by a dagger thrown from a mountain-top by Owain in a fit of temper Even in those days the locals would dream up the craziest stories in order to attract tourists.

One undisputed fact is that Owain was declared Prince of Wales in 1400 by his supporters and that 529 years later the first Urdd Eisteddfod was held.

Denbigh (Dinbych)

Many guide books have described Denbigh as a rural town where sheep provide the main income. This is inaccurate. When you visit the place just count the number of sheep you spot buying anything.

The town can boast to being the burial place or the birthplace of at least two famous Welshmen – one a name known throughout Wales; another throughout the world. Twm o'r Nant was an eighteenth-century playwright regarded as the Welsh Shakespeare. The other was Henry

Morton Stanley who uttered those immortal words: "Dr Livingstone, I presume", in the middle of the jungle. Considering the good doctor was the only other white person within approximately 2000 miles of Stanley, that was a fair assumption.

Dolgellau

A town of narrow streets with (don't tell me – yes, a castle built by Edward I – or, at least, he supervised it). The imposing mountain, Cader Idris, looms over the town – all 2,927 feet of it, or whatever that is in metres. There is a story that whoever spends the night on the highest peak will wake up on the morning transformed either to a poet or a madman. Surely anyone who decides to spend the night on the peak was mad to start with. If you have more material desires than visiting the nearby Cymer Abbey (*Abaty Cymer*) founded by the Cistercians in 1199, you can try your luck at prospecting for gold in one of the many Mawddach valley streams. Gold from these parts has been used for the majority of the Windsor dynasty's wedding rings – so the precious material must be cursed so, on second thoughts, best to leave your pan at home.

A group of Quakers from here founded the settlement of Pennsylvania in 1686 led by one Rowland Ellis and the well-known college of Bryn Mawr in the USA is named after its Welsh counterpart.

Holyhead (Caergybi)

This is a ferry terminal carrying passengers to and from Ireland. On a clear day, standing on the top of the local mountain, you can see the Emerald Isle, the Isle of Man (which disproves the theory that no man is an island), Snowdon (*Eryri*) and the Cumbrian peaks. Ornithologists/bird-watchers/twitchers/anoraks ignore such sights and prefer to look downwards to the cliffs around South Stack lighthouse where myriads of sea-birds teem during the nesting season. Bird-watchers can look at birds all year round because they don't have a mating or nesting season.

Holywell (Treffynnon)

This old town overlooking the Dee estuary was named after the well which it is said sprang up at the very spot where St Winefride (Gwenfrewi) lost her head (literally) after she stoutly defended her honour from a lustful squire by the name of Caradog (What a cad!). This behaviour – possibly unusual by today's standards) is why Holywell ranks as one of the seven wonders of Wales.

Llandudno

Feeling low because you're getting on a bit? Then why not visit this lovely town by the sea? You'll probably be the youngest there. Standing on top of either of the two hills – the Great Orme and the Little Orme – you will espy a sea of white. This is not foam. It's the collective hairdos of well-groomed ladies eagerly anticipating the next round of bingo. There is a pleasant arts centre near the shingle beach and a few pubs, bars and restaurants – even a club for the under 60s which attracts coach loads of youngsters from far away places like England.

Llanfair-pwllgwyngyll-go-ger-y-chwyrndrobwll-llantysilio-go-go-goch

Certain cynical Welsh patriots have translated this very long place name as 'Birmingham-by-the-sea'. This is by no means an accurate translation as it omits reference to many other parts of the Midlands. In fact, the name refers to the churches associated with two saints – Mair and Tysilio.

By any standards this is an extremely long-winded place name so it is often shortened to 'Llanfair PG' in order to accommodate its name on envelopes and road signs. The full name is marginally longer than the train station which bears its name.

A mile or two from the village are the Menai Straits on whose banks dwelt the famous artist Kyffin Williams and where you will find a statue of Nelson looking out to sea. Another landmark of the village is the Marquess of Anglesey's Column and it is possible to walk up the 115 steps.

Oh yes – an English translation of the name is 'St Mary's church in the hollow of the white hazel near to the rapid whirlpool and the church of St Tysilio of the red cave'. This could count as an early sat nav direction.

Llangollen

Every year the International Eisteddfod is held in this quaint little town. Pavarotti sang here in a choir. Flowers fill the stage and in the good weather, the colourful outfits of dancers and singers festoon the streets – with, of course, the contestants still wearing them.

Llangollen Bridge, with its unequal pointed arches, is listed among the seven Wonders of Wales. At Pontcysyllte near the town is Thomas Telford's aqueduct, a cast-iron trough supported on nineteen stone pillars and carrying the canal at a height of 126 feet above the Dee valley.

At the eisteddfod's main pavilion there are evening concerts for those who prefer ballet to Butlins or Puccini to Pontins.

Rhyl

Its name rhymes with 'thrill', so visitors will not be surprised to find this small town is even livelier than resorts in England such as Eastbourne and the Chelsea pensioners'

barracks. The famous Sun Centre has a roof over it so that no-one can be harmed by the sun – rather like a ski resort without any snow. That's lateral thinking for you!

Many visitors from across the water have chosen to settle here and live out their days cavorting on the Funfair, Fun Maze and Family Fun centre. Yes – it's all non-stop fun in Rhyl, so you are advised to bring some Valium with you in case you become over-excited.

Sorry. No cakes left. I ate them all.

St Asaph (Llanelwy)

Here you will find the smallest cathedral in Britain. Perhaps congregations were even smaller in days gone by. Here there are monuments to Bishop William Morgan, William Salesbury, Bishop Richard Davies and Thomas Huet who together were responsible for translating both the Old and New Testaments into Welsh in the mid-sixteenth century. The English poet Gerard Manley Hopkins lived in this part of Wales in the nineteenth century and some of his poetry shows an attempt to embody different Welsh verse forms in an English context.

Wrexham (Wrecsam)

Another of the Seven Wonders of Wales belongs to this town – the Wrexham Steeple atop St Giles church. Elihu Yale was born here and a replica of the steeple has been incorporated into the university buildings of Yale in Connecticut.

Apart from this feature, the other wonder is why anyone would want to come here, However, if your taste in architecture can accommodate both traditional nondescript and modern featurelessness you will wallow in the town's ordinariness. Beauty, as we know, is in the eyes of the beholder so, as you walk around, don't keep your contact lenses in.

Llanuwchllyn

If you wanted to be cruel, Llanuwchllyn could best be described as a one-horse town where someone shot the horse. But this modest little settlement at the southern end of Bala lake is one of the cradles of Welsh culture. As you turn into the village, you'll notice two statues – O. M. Edwards and Ifan ab Owen Edwards, father and son of this parish – whose contribution to the Welsh way of life is almost immeasurable. Between them they revolutionised education, founded Welsh children's magazines and founded Urdd Gobaith Cymru (Welsh League of Youth). At Glan-llyn, two miles away, children from all over Wales gather for the Urdd summer school.

Llanystumdwy

Visitors to this enchanted village will no doubt be drawn there by the spell of that great Welsh statesman David Lloyd George – who was actually born in England. Many called him the 'Welsh wizard' probably because he miraculously changed himself from a fervent Welsh Nationalist into a royalist sycophant within a matter of a few years. This amazing metamorphosis set a trend for other Welsh politicians who, once elected to Parliament, performed quite stunning sleights of hand.

Two notable examples – one in Plaid Cymru and the other in the Labour party – suffered traumatic bouts of amnesia by forgetting their original commitment to socialism and being exalted to a seat in the House of Lords. But more of that later.

Porthmadog

This scenic harbour is billed as the gateway to Snowdonia National Park. Once a great seaport and boasting a steam railway, the place attracts many a yacht owner from England. Wales, as we have noted, is used to invasions and, indeed, Welsh people themselves are not averse to migrating to other lands. One of the most famous emigrants was Madog who, according to somewhat biased folklore perhaps, left the shores of Wales back in the 12th century and discovered America. Sceptics argue that Madog probably got no further than Ireland. Whoever actually discovered America remains a contentious issue – perhaps it was a Scot called Macdonald.

Another well-known traveller – Lawrence of Arabia – was born in nearby Tremadog.

Pwllheli

One authoritative linguistic source tells us that "The pronunciation of Pwllheli includes a sound not heard in the English language" – this sound being "a voiceless alveolar lateral fricative". The natives of this town have lived all this time without realising how clever they are. The sound is probably not heard in Swahili and Latvian but visitors from Africa and the Baltic should not be discouraged from travelling to Pwllheli. For here, especially in the summer, they will be able to spot jolly holidaymakers from Liverpool and Birmingham relishing in the *haute cuisine* offered by Butlins – a well-established holiday camp specialising in burgers and chips, bangers (sausages) and chips, chips with more chips. Here glamorous grannies –some as old as 45 – strut their stuff. The more athletic campers can enjoy a game of pool or darts.

Let us not condemn our Midland cousins for the 'ritual murder of vowels' as the poet R. S. Thomas, who lived nearby, once wrote. Most indigenous Welsh people in the north of the nation are bilingual and can even interpret from Brummie into English if required.

Trawsfynydd

For something a little bit different try Trawsfynydd. Here stands the first inland nuclear power station in Britain. At night

Pity this hotel has no windows. The view is great.

Trawsfynydd has its own aurora borealis as the mountain sheep glow in truly Jacob-like coats of many colours. Two centre holidays can be arranged as Trawsfynydd is now twinned with Chernobyl.

Tryweryn

A veritable beauty spot dedicated to the thirsty denizens of some large settlement in England. A village inhabited by a Welsh-speaking population was drowned in order to supply the precious fluid. Ironically, hardly anyone now drinks water from taps but the old outmoded tradition of washing in tap water still prevails in a few outlying parts of the UK. Another Welsh valley – Clywedog – suffered the same fate. Strange – since Manchester is reputed to suffer perpetual rainfall. Perhaps, if Wales suffers a drought, the Manchester United and Manchester City football grounds could be drowned and the water pumped to Wales. No doubt the Mancunians would not object to reciprocating in this way.

MID WALES

Brecon (Aberhonddu)

Brecon's claim to fame is its annual jazz festival which attracts many a bald-headed and usually bearded man trailing a pony tail. There is music on the streets, in large tents, in hotels and in the town hall. Beer flows down necks and abandoned chip bags flow down the streets. There is hardly a need for a large police presence because jazz enthusiasts are 'cool' and prefer real ale to lager.

The town is uninspiring but there is an arts centre with café alongside the river. Journeying from south of the country, travellers will pass through the Brecon Beacons punctuated by mobile caffs offering homely fare such as bacon baps and sausage sandwiches, both of which tend to make the consumer's bowels also quite mobile.

Clywedog Reservoir

High in the mountains west of Lanidloes, along the mountain road to Machynlleth, lies the large reservoir of Clywedog. Many deep and largely inaccessible valleys were drowned in the 1960s to form the lake, owned by Birmingham Corporation. Motorists should be wary when parking in a lay-by to enjoy the view down below. Faulty brakes could result in your vehicle – with or without you in it – cascading gently into the lake. This would be a tragedy because the good people of Birmingham would then have to filter the water before using it.

The Elan Valley (*Cwm Elan*) also supplies water to Birmingham at no cost while here, as at Tryweryn, local people for some time had no piped water. The obvious answer was to move to Birmingham but many old-fashioned and stubborn residents mysteriously preferred boring unspoilt scenery to the bustle and smoke of Brum – how typically Welsh.

Crickhowell

There is a noble lord who takes his title from this small town. One Nicholas Edwards, once Secretary of State for Wales, adopted the name on his elevation to the Upper House. This is interesting because his constituency was in Pembrokeshire. Many Tory ministers – but not all – are not noted for their in-depth knowledge of Wales even though they might have been voted in to represent a Welsh constituency so perhaps Mr Edwards truly believed that Crickhowell was in Pembrokeshire.

The Bear Hotel in the town was at one time well-known for its landlady who preceded and exceeded Basil Fawlty in the caustic and bad-tempered way in which she greeted would-be customers. She was, in her inimitable way, as politically incorrect as the noble lord.

Llandrindod Wells

Here is the veritable Mecca for Meetings, notably at the once dilapidated Metropole Hotel.

Now refurbished to bring it up to mid 20th century standards, the hotel graces the main road. Visitors to this quiet town should not plan for a prolonged visit since a tour of the shops has been timed as an average of 17 minutes from start to finish.

The place is full of mystery. The ten-yearly census confirms that there are still people actually living – or at least existing there but to the inexperienced eye it is the veritable Mary Celeste of Wales. It could be its Eighth Wonder. Perchance you will glimpse the furtive fluttering of lace curtains in the window of an erstwhile fashionable dwelling or perhaps hear the distant drone of guests snoring as they sit in the lounge of a B&B.

And what is that creature rising from the depths of the lake in the park? Is it a dragon? A fish? Or discarded trolley? Each year there is a Victorian Festival when locals dust off their Sunday best and regale themselves in authentic costumes of that distant era. So tourists – have your striped blazer dry-cleaned and your bustled dress de-

mothballed. This is your opportunity to merge into the somnolent gaiety of the festival.

Llanelwedd

We have noted the fact that this 'suburb' of Builth Wells stages each year the Royal Welsh Agricultural Show. Take the usual precautions against animals cooped in for too long. However,

two additional pieces of information might be helpful. First, don't be alarmed if you have to abandon your vehicle some distance from the showground. There is a regular bus service to take you from the parking areas to the event. The only snag is, you might have to start queuing for a parking space anything up to five miles away, so bring a packed lunch and thermos flask. Secondly, check your bank balance before you start out. The admission fee could give you a severe pain in the wallet. Best to bring a walking stick if you are under 65 and pretend you're a pensioner or crawl below the height of the kiosk window and get in free. Don't try this if it's muddy.

Llangurig

The village has two claims to fame. It is the first village on the River Wye as it flows from its source in the mountains of Pumlumon and at 1,000 feet it is reputed to be the highest village in Wales. It is generally accepted also as the exact centre of Wales, although, in view of its rather sleepy atmosphere, it should perhaps be known as the 'dead centre'.

The parish church was founded in around 550 AD as some of the older residents well remember at first hand. It has been renovated over many centuries and is probably due for further work to turn it into a bingo hall or retail warehouse.

Llanidloes

This sleepy market town woke up in 1839 for a short but well-documented Chartist rebellion before hitting the snooze button to rest some more. The interesting market hall is slap-bang in the middle of a crossroads. Perhaps, to ease congestion, it should be removed stone by stone and shifted to the museum at St Fagan's. It's doubtful whether anyone would notice.

Machynlleth

Here in the Dyfi valley is the picturesque setting for Owain Glyndŵr's Welsh Parliament and the more enduring empire of Laura Ashley, although this mega-store has now moved its headquarters. There was much discussion that the capital of Wales should have been Machynlleth instead of Cardiff but since very few members of the Government at that time knew where Wales was, let alone Machynlleth, Cardiff had a head start, since most people had heard of Tiger Bay and Shirley Bassey.

Just a couple of miles north of Machynlleth is the Centre for Alternative Technology (*Canolfan y Dechnoleg Amgen*). This was developed some years ago when Wales was becoming 'green' while the rest of Britain was still blue and occasionally red. Here you can see energy being generated in various novel ways. For example, ten male voice choirs singing in rota throughout twenty four hours direct their voices to a large wheel which is then turned over cogs. This, in turn, propels another wheel in the same building – a converted electricity sub-station – which activates a robot constructed entirely out of recycled gas cookers. The robot advances holding a crude stick in either hand down a ramp towards a

redundant coal-merchant who – on receipt of the two sticks – rubs them vigorously together thus creating a spark which is directed towards a candle made of organically produced beeswax. The candle is then ignited.

This entirely 'green' and alternative operation lasts for the duration of one rendering of 'Men of Harlech' which – discounting encores and breaks for beer – amounts to twenty three minutes. In one day, therefore, a total of sixty two and a half candles are set alight. In terms of power, this would be sufficient to heat five microwave

No luxury is spared to attract tourists.

suppers for two or to defrost three members of Merched y Wawr – a body of worthy matrons akin to the WI but who pose naked in Welsh.

Windmills, watermills and solar panels are also to be seen at the centre as well as innovative methods of insulating houses such as constructing them entirely out of polystyrene disposable beakers or filling the lofts with all-purpose chicken manure; this stops heat from escaping through the roof while at the same time ensuring a good crop of home-grown mushrooms. The manure can also be used to power alternative vehicle engines, encourage hair growth (already tested successfully on balding middle-aged male hamsters) and as a particularly piquant relish on veggie burgers.

Visitors to the centre may wish to visit the site shop where souvenirs are on sale. Edible sandals and bio-degradable miners' lamps are just two of the reasonably-priced articles for sale. In the not too distant future, visitors to Wales will notice rows of terraced houses with glass roofs (known in posher places as 'conservatories') with satellite dishes that can also be used as woks.

Newtown (Y Drenewydd)

This is the town where Robert Owen (1771-1858) lived – the man whose vision of a socialist Utopia bore fruit in factory reform and the creation of a Cooperative Movement. He is buried, along with any real socialist dreams, in a derelict graveyard. The town itself is appropriately modest and really the only new thing about the place is its name.

Offa's Dyke (Clawdd Offa)

Stretching over a considerable length as a kind of fortification, this ditch and wall was probably built to keep the marauding Welsh out of Mercia and other parts of England ruled over by King Offa in the eighth century AD. Considering the hordes of Welsh people who crossed the border over the centuries the dyke didn't appear to work. That's because the Welsh invented wellies. No piddling little ditch was going to keep them away from shopping at Harrods.

Rhayader (Rhaeadr Gwy)

Rhayader claims to be the oldest town in Wales dating back to the 5th century. Neolithic remains have also been found but presumably, in those days, Rhayader was more of a mound than a town. Its Welsh name is *Rhaeadr Gwy* – which means 'waterfall on the Wye'. This is also 'the first town on the Wye' according to official records, so Llangurig could be the first depending on which direction you are coming from. Rhayader is the gateway to the drowned Elan valley and the Romans, monks and drovers regularly passed this way.

The town's main claim to uniqueness is that there is free parking in the town and since it is only two hours from Cardiff, Manchester and Birmingham it could well become a commuter's paradise.

Sennybridge (Pontsenni)

Here, not far from Brecon, is a large tract of boggy moorland dedicated to Army training. The surrounding area, we are told, is 'thinly populated'. Perhaps the odd stray bullet might account for this. There are, however, many species of animals: fox, rabbits, and armour-plated sheep. Tanks tend to be filled with soldiers rather than fish and, although far from sea, the occasional shell can be found along with the indigenous fossilised mortar bombs.

When the red flag is flying walking parties are advised not to go bog snorkelling.

Welshpool (Y Trallwng)

This is the most northerly town in mid-Wales. There are good road and rail links so it is quite easy to get away unless you are an avid garden-visitor, in which case Powys Castle is a must. The gardens there were renovated by Capability Brown in the 19th century. If you are not an avid garden-visitor there are good road and rail links.

Aberaeron

What a pretty place. Georgian houses of various hues face the small harbour where, long ago, ships were built. Aberaeron has become a fashionable place to eat and stay and even to film glossy Welsh soaps. There are coastal walks and festivals to enjoy, including the Welsh Ponies and Cobs Festival and the Seafood Festival. Not much singing and dancing goes on at these two events but the lingering aroma of manure and cockles is enough to stimulate the most jaded nostril.

Aberystwyth

A university by the sea stands here and the National Library of Wales, which keeps a copy of every book in print. It's a strange town with a student population that's equal in number to the local one so it will feel very different (and pleasantly relaxing) if you plan your visit for outside the academic terms.

Like a few other beaches in Wales, there are hazards for those tourists who enjoy splashing about in the sea. Four flags fly on the sand, each one giving a different message. Flag 1: 'Safe bathing for those equipped with a wet suit, diver's helmet and an underdeveloped sense of smell'. Flag 2: 'Avoid bathing unless you wish to emerge from the water looking as though you have just acquired an instant tan'. Flag 3: 'Not advised unless your sense of fun is bobsleighing through sewage pipes'. Flag 4: 'The sea is so dirty even the waves won't come in'.

To compensate for the relative lack of bathing opportunities (best to have a dip at night when you can't see the colour of the water) tourism relies heavily on the number of pubs. No need to go on a pub crawl. The pubs are so close together some have got adjoining doors. Ancient relics here include the castle, the pier, and several of the human variety who have struggled across the road from their communal homes to

A mid-summer's day in Aberystwyth

enjoy breathing – not the invigorating ozone – just breathing.

Borth (Y Borth)

Like the stoat and the ermine, Borth is a different animal in summer and winter. Summer sees the village groaning under the weight of full caravan parks. Water-skiing is popular but not everyone is rich enough to hire a boat to tow them so specially-bred amphibious donkeys can be hired to tug you at a slightly slower pace.

A re-furbished toilet with a sea view

In winter it's a different story. Since most of the houses are second homes, the main streets in December resemble Dodge City when the James brothers were in town, Not that there's a lot to venture out for since the local amenities amount to one chip shop and a public toilet. But you might still be able to get into the small zoo (called an 'animalarium', note the posh English influence). The richest resident is the entrepreneur who produces 'closed' signs for the local traders.

Cardigan (Aberteifi)

Situated on the Teifi estuary, Cardigan is a town with several quaint Georgian and Victorian houses. Here a plaque commemorates the fact that the very first National Eisteddfod was held here in 1176. There was a small gap after that for a few hundred years while the adjudicators sorted out the scoring system. The old castle walls (pity there are no new castles dotted around) are held in place by steel girders.

For many visitors, the prospect of meeting

dolphins is an attractive idea but in this part of Wales the sea-life is Welsh-speaking so, in order to communicate, it's advisable to buy from the town's main bookstore, a Welsh–English Dolphin Dictionary. It's very cheap as there are not many words in it.

Carmarthen (Caerfyrddin)

This is a market town with fine castle walls that once protected a Welsh princess. The old Arthurian legend proclaimed that if the old oak tree that stood for centuries in the town should ever fall, then the town would sink into the sea. Not long ago the tree was removed. Carmarthen is still above sea-level but Wrexham suffered an earthquake and Tywyn in north Wales was flooded. Merlin the wizard was said to have been born in a cave near to the town. Nowadays he could have applied for a council house.

Devil's Bridge (Pontarfynach)

High in the foothills of the Cambrian Mountains you will find this small village noted for being the terminus of the Vale of Rheidol steam-line. The journey is spectacular on the narrow gauge track. Its three bridges are above each other, crossing a narrow gorge where the river Mynach meets the Rheidol. The lowest bridge dates back to the Middle Ages. Built by the monks of Strata Florida Abbey, the name in English seems strangely inappropriate, but the nearby waterfalls form a seething cauldron of fierce white water known as the Devil's Punchbowl. Standing there, watching this miracle of nature, you begin to realise that there are more amazing things for tourists to see than burger outlets and hot dog stands.

Fishguard (Abergwaun)

Lower Fishguard was the setting for the 1971 film of *Under Milk Wood*. It was here that a French force landed with nearly 1400 troops. The purpose of the invasion in 1797 has never been clarified. Some historians say that they were blown off course on their way to Ireland but there is no record of any rugby international having been arranged in that year. Whatever the reason, the French invaders were repelled – and probably repulsed – by a hastily marshalled group of women dressed in Welsh costume, brandishing huge leeks and chanting some very early Dafydd Iwan songs.

There must be something about this relatively unimpressive location because the film *Moby Dick* was also shot here.

Haverfordwest (Hwlffordd)

Basking in the dubious glory of being known as 'Little England beyond Wales', the town appears as a bastion of Englishness. To the north of the town lies the Welsh equivalent of the equator – the Landsker, an invisible line which divides the Welsh-speaking north of old Pembrokeshire from the Anglicised south.

This is no reflection on the good citizens of the town, but one interpretation of 'Haverfordwest' is 'the ford used by fat cows'. In 1348 – it might have been a Tuesday – the town was ravaged by the Black Death. Why this particular spot was chosen is not known but since this type of event is likely to occur every 700 years or so, visitors are advised to sport an airtight mask while walking the hilly streets.

Lampeter (Llanbedr Pont Steffan)

This is a small university town with a college that was once dedicated exclusively to theological studies. It offers some up-market shops – sorry, 'boutiques' – but little else. If this seems to be a somewhat churlish assessment of Lampeter's charms and attractions, official tourist information lists Chamber of Trade and Town Council meetings as the highspots in the calendar.

Llandeilo

This market town attracts thousands of visitors a year because it is located close to the National Botanic Garden of Wales. This was built on the site of a mansion owned by the Middleton family who lived there in the 1600s. In 1789 William Paxton bought the estate and installed probably the earliest WC in Wales. Centuries later most of the houses in the south Wales valleys did not possess one. Unfortunately, the house burnt down in 1931 and the Garden opened in the year 2000. There is a huge glasshouse occupied by exotic plants.

Nearby, stand the impressive remains of Carreg Cennen, a castle built by... (yes, you're right) the ruined abbey of Talyllychau and the remains of Roman gold-mining operations at Dolaucothi. What a feast of ancient relics for the visitor to take in. A trip to the town of Llandeilo might seem an anti-climax but Llandeilo – like some other towns in west Wales – is growing in sophistication – particularly with regard to its cuisine. Delicacies such as sausage in batter and potato fritters are being replaced by even more elegant menus.

Llandovery (Llanymddyfri)

Llandovery, like Llandeilo and many other towns

in Wales, is a market town that attracts many tourists. It is surrounded by three rivers and is said to still retain a mediaeval atmosphere. This is difficult to substantiate since, as far as the most recent Census shows, no-one over the age of 600 actually lives in the town.

However, there is a fairly old public school here and a plethora of pubs – if that's the correct collective term. A charter by Richard III designated the place as the only locality to have the right to establish taverns. A public school and lots of pubs – could there be a more obvious connection?

Near to the town the greatest Welsh hymn-writer – William Williams of Pantycelyn saw out his days. Ever since then, hymn-singing has been part of the Welsh way of life featuring in the repertoire of male voice choirs and rosy-faced rugby supporters.

Llanelli

From this unpretentious town has come a war chant that has struck fear into the hearts of foreign rugby supporters. Even the mighty All Blacks succumbed to its devastating symbolism. Forget the *haka*. *'Sosban fach'* rendered by a mass of Llanelli Scarlets fans is worth at least six points before the game begins. And who would not shake as these words are bellowed out in a ferocious crescendo: *'the little saucepan is boiling on the fire'* and *'the cat has scratched little Johnny'*.

As the noted Anglo-Welsh poet Harri Webb proclaimed: 'Sing a song of rugby – buttocks, booze and blood'. It is not quite clear how buttocks feature here but there is certainly a link between rugby and booze in Llanelli because an influential incomer from Lancashire – the Reverend James Buckley – managed to found a brewery in the 1770s or at least, the brewery was named after him. Now his name lives on in a brew produced by Brains in Cardiff.

Llangrannog

In the 2001 Census a total of 772 persons were recorded as living in this small coastal village. This number is greatly increased during the times when young people attend the Urdd activity camps where the atmosphere is somewhere between scouts, girl guides and Stalag 17. This influx of youth possibly accounts for the production of home-made ice-cream on sale. The famous English composer Edward Elgar spent a holiday here but no-one knows why.

The area has also attracted hordes of hippies, or whatever the modern tag is to describe them.

Nant-y-moch

The reservoir at Nant-y-moch is one of those rare specimens in Wales – it wasn't built to supply water to England. It nevertheless drowned one of the few remaining Welsh wildernesses and used all the arguments so prevalent in such cases – 'it'll look nice'; 'we'll build new roads'; there's nothing there really'. Built to generate hydro-electric power in 1964 the stretch of water lies near to where Owain Glyndŵr's army gained a famous victory over the troops of Henry IV.

Newcastle Emlyn (Castell Newydd Emlyn)

If your interest in coracles has led you to this part of Wales, it's because you have discovered that the National Coracle Centre is situated nearby.

In this small town there is also a childhood Museum featuring dolls, dolls houses and teddy bears. If this sounds rather gender-biased, no doubt there are also model trains, lead soldiers and rows of ancient, winning conkers. The village of Adpar, separated from the town only by a bridge, lays claim to being the location of the first printing press in Wales. This is probably more authentic than the odd few hundred or so pianos in various parts of Wales on which the Welsh national anthem was composed.

New Quay (Ceinewydd)

Blatantly touristified – caravan parks, holiday parks, hotels and guest-houses have sprung up like germinating mustard seeds. Pack the usual holiday accessories but leave one case aside for crampons, ropes and climbing boots – those streets are steep! The harbour is full of boats so it's important if you moor your craft here to

make it stand out so that you can identify it after the winter season is over. Polka dots and tiger stripes were in last year.

The local council's award-winning Xmas decotations

Pembroke (Penfro)

The town has a magnificent castle and some inviting pubs. The family of Haggar ran a cinema here for decades. There are limited shops and cafés in the main street but you can take a brief journey to Pembroke Dock where there are even fewer shops and cafés. Before the linking bridge was built a short ferry crossing was a delightful way to cross over to Haverfordwest. It is not all that long ago when a German Panzer division was stationed here. As a result inter-breeding with the locals has produced some quaintly named children, such as Fritz von Wilhelm ap Robat and Heidi Ribbentropp-Davies.

Pendine (Pentywyn)

If your idea of a sparkling holiday is to rub shoulders with people in caravans nestling twixt a cluster of souvenir shops this is your bit of paradise. The beach is 7 miles long. While many remember or have heard of the heroic attempts by Sir Donald Campbell to beat the world land-

57

speed record, very very few could honestly say they have a clue who one J. G. Parry-Thomas was. He too held the world land-speed record and deserves some recognition because Campbell needed a car to break the record whereas dear old J. G. (we are unreliably told) achieved it running in bare feet – and that's a tricky thing to do on wet sand.

Preseli (Y Preselau)

Geological surveyors have proved that the stones used to erect Stonehenge in Wiltshire came from an outcrop in this area. But there are plenty of mini-cromlechs draping the slopes. What is not certain is whether they also took a few ancient druids with them, like those who dress up at Eisteddfod time.

St David's (Tyddewi)

A couple of tea rooms and a cathedral set in a hollow – that's St David's. But the general area around the 'smallest city in Wales, demands attention. Walkers and pedallists will revel in the surrounding countryside. But, on the other hand, nearly the whole of Wales – with so much unspoiled and impressive contrasts of mountains and lakes – is an invitation to park the car and stretch those two pegs normally used for changing gear and controlling the throttle.

Strata Florida (Ystrad-fflur)

'The way of flowers' has been referred to as the 'Westminster of Wales' in respect of the abbey located here. There are, however, some slight differences. The roof has long gone as are most of the walls, while the cross shape formed by the outer walls is barely visible. This is not surprising when you consider that it was struck by lightning and burned by our old and noble friend Eddie the One when he was trying to assert his authority over the naughty Welsh nationalists.

Tradition has it that the great Welsh poet and troubadour, Dafydd ap Gwilym, is buried in the shadow of a yew tree within its grounds.

Tenby (Dinbych-y-pysgod)

This picturesque walled town offers the holiday-maker a variety of activities. There is a fine harbour, two sandy beaches and some notable buildings such as the Tudor Merchant's house and an interesting museum. In this building you can listen to the familiar sounds of Wales – from the raucous cry of seagulls as they dip into Tenby Harbour to the crunch of pigeons underfoot on Hayes Island in Cardiff, or the quaint spewing sound of teenagers in most city streets at the weekend.

The real surprise is that in Tenby – unlike most seaside resorts in the UK, not just Wales – you can actually find a restaurant menu which doesn't have chips with every dish. So Benidorm or Magaluf it is not! You can even buy mead made by the monks of the nearby Caldy Island so this is definitely a resort that belies its first impressions.

Tregaron

Human visitors are always welcome in this small town in west Wales. But the most welcome visitor is the red kite which is making something of a come-back in this area. Immigrants from England have also nested here and an annual count indicates that they are not yet in danger of extinction. The town is perhaps best known for its extensive peat bog (Cors Caron) to the north but it also boasts two famous sons. Henry Richard stands in the town's main square or, at least, a statue of him. He was known as the 'Apostle of Peace' for his work with the Peace Union, the Victorian forerunner of the United Nations.

Peace was not high on the agenda of the other celebrity – Thomas Jones, or Twm Siôn Cati, a sixteenth-century highwayman. This local Dick Turpin introduced the custom now practised in the organically-conscious settlement of Tegaron where ecologically-correct shoppers pay exorbitant prices for carrots cultivated in recycled bath-water and cheese made from the milk of free-range buffalo.

SOUTH WALES

Aberdare (Aberdâr)

Like many of the former heavy industry towns in south Wales, Aberdare boasts of what it once was rather than what it now has to offer residents and visitors alike. Iron and coal were the catalysts for the town's initial expansion, although Aberdare is one of the oldest settlements in the south Wales valleys. Once there were boats on the lake, thriving chapels and a cinema. Today the town's claim to fame is that the actor Ioan Gruffydd was born here. It is not known whether he ever came back once he had made it in Hollywood but he probably did, or does, because valleys people tend to remain valleys people and that is this region's charm.

Abergavenny (Y Fenni)

This pleasant market town in the Usk valley basks in the title of the 'Gateway to Wales' which is rooted deep in the historical fact that most English invasions were centred on this area. By today, it's difficult to tell that you're in Wales at all. Standing in the shadow of four strangely-named mountains – the Skirrid, the Little Skirrid, the Sugar Loaf and Blorenge – the dearth of Welsh speakers makes it difficult to believe that during the last century the town was an important centre in a growing movement to revive traditional Welsh culture. This was mainly due to the efforts of Lord and Lady Llanover, but when the lord passed away, so did the annual eisteddfod which drew the cream of the Welsh literati to the area.

The farmer's market and a monthly covered market are attractive events. A former pop star wrote a song called 'Taking a trip up to Abergavenny' – so enchanted was he by the town's name. We await similar tributes in popular mode to Llandrindod and Llanfairpwll etc.

Barry (Y Barri)

The rural peace of Barry was shattered in the 1840s when work started on building the town's first dock – a tribute to the importance of the coal-mining valleys of the Rhondda.

Barry Island is really the centre of activities for the visitor rather than the rather featureless town. There is a sandy beach, some shades lighter than the sea that brings in exciting flotsam and jetsam – sea shells, sewage and, in times past, the occasional body of an unhappy inmate of the nearby holiday camp, dashed on the rocks while trying to escape.

The fun fair is well laid out and carefully planned. After you've paid half a week's wages for two hot dogs, a stick of candy floss and a carton of whelks you can spend the other half on the roller-coaster or big wheel, and having emptied your stomach and your wallet, you can use your credit card for a round of jumbo sausages and chips and so on until you get a rare experience of perpetual motions.

Bridgend (Pen-y-bont)

This lively little town lies to the west of the affluent Vale of Glamorgan. During shopping hours you will note that every young woman under the age of 21 has a fashion accessory, namely a baby – or two. Teenage pregnancies are a social occasion here, rather like the *bar mitzvah* among the Jewish communities around the world.

Just outside the town is a large shopping centre. The village of Laleston a mile or two away offers some attractive public houses but be careful driving around this area as the headquarters of the South Wales Police employs people who are expert in capturing errant motorists on camera. You can then buy your picture for a few pounds and send it to friends as a novelty postcard.

Caerleon

This small village is a former site of a Roman encampment. It is a few miles away from Newport but a thousand light-years away as far as atmosphere is concerned. The clear remains of an amphitheatre, barracks and villas will appeal to tourists although some residents of many years haven't bothered to walk a few steps to go and see the sights. The poet Tennyson stayed here in his quest for knowledge about the Arthurian legend but his theory that the amphitheatre was really Arthur's round table suggests he had drunk a little too much of the local brew. Caerleon has probably the largest number of pubs per square metre in Wales. This was obviously the reason why Caesar's lads came here in the first place.

Caerphilly (Caerffili)

Caerphilly equals cheese and the castle. In fact, every summer the local council organises a Big Cheese Festival just outside the castle grounds. The castle is the second largest in Britain, next to the pile in Windsor – the castle, not the Royal family. The castle's unique feature is its leaning tower which lists at a greater angle than the one in Pisa. Recent research, however, has proved that the tower is perfectly perpendicular and that the whole of Caerphilly is subsiding at an acute angle and sliding inexorably into the moat. Underwater shopping at the town's Co-op could well be a major touristy attraction in years to come.

Cardiff (Caerdydd)

Cardiff – like Swansea and Newport – has had much of its former docks area transformed by planners and estate agents. You can't buy flats here; they're called 'apartments' which are described in the jargon as 'executive' (over-priced); 'convenient' (next door to the railway station'); in the 'marina' (near a bit of polluted water with a few boats on it).

Cardiff Castle is a major attraction. Its ornate interior decoration – like its smaller version at nearby Castell Coch – cunningly combines ostentation with sumptuous vulgarity – rather like the mediaeval banquets held there.

But where better to appreciate the history and culture of Wales than at the National Museum

Free Wales Army hero inspects the local talent.

in the impressive environs of the civic centre. Not that the museum is filled exclusively with Welsh exhibits. The art gallery is noted for its fine collection of world-renowned artists' contributions to the visual aesthete. Some of the old masters provoke animated debate among experts. Are they really from the brush of Rubens? Or were they part of a collection of masterpieces given away free in a breakfast cereal promotion? Why not go and see them and make up your own mind.

The Millennium Stadium and Millennium Centre stand boldly, symbolising the regeneration of the city as a truly cosmopolitan conurbation. You can even listen to the sounds of nature here: the murmuring of the *Big Issue* sellers; the cooing of pigeons; the warbling of street musicians and the bellowing of supporters as Cardiff City actually score a goal.

Chepstow (Cas-gwent)

Chepstow Castle is reputed to be the oldest surviving stone fortification in Britain. William the Conqueror ordered its construction in 1067 in order to prevent the Welsh from attacking Gloucestershire, though why those rampaging Welsh would want to attack that part of England is not known; they didn't even have any decent cheese in those days.

The Welsh Grand National is held at the racecourse, attracting that curious breed who are all too ready and willing to put their shirts (and blouses for that matter) on a temperamental and rarely trustworthy beast.

Cwmbrân

Five miles north of Newport lies Cwmbrân – an example of that much-heralded concept of the new way of life back in the 1960s and onwards – the 'new town'. The main characteristics of a new town are well-planned streets and estates, acres of car parking space, millions of unsightly bricks and a pedestrianised town centre, at least in some places. When you have parked your car, hopefully free of charge, you discover the catch – apart from the regulation global chain stores, there's absolutely nothing to keep you there. In Cwmbrân, the wind whistles down the corridors of the shopping areas as if to say: 'You've been here long enough; now go home.'

Cowbridge (Y Bont-faen)

In London, those with more money than sense (landed gentry, pop stars, diplomats and Hooray

Henrys) make a bee-line for Knightsbridge. The Cardiff equivalent is Cowbridge. Anything bought in this town, which is about 12 miles west of the capital, reeks of exclusivity. But if you can cope with imagining that you have stepped out of Wales and into Surrey, there is much to commend about Cowbridge. The pubs have character and serve good real ale and food; there is jazz in the streets in the summer and you are unlikely to be robbed of your mobile phone because every child born here has one as a christening present. So forget your working class roots and enjoy the experience of feeling/being middle-class. Revel in the absence of street beggars: *The Big Issue* is not a big issue here.

Craig-y-nos

This small village at the head of the Swansea Valley owes its fame to something completely different from the coal-mining heritage of the rest of the area. It was to Craig-y-Nos Castle that famed operatic prima donna Adelina Patti fled for refuge from the bright lights of success –and

you can't get much further than this. She bought the castle in 1871 and spent part of her lavish fortune on improving it, including installing her own private theatre.

After her death in 1919, the castle was gifted to the Welsh National Memorial Association and converted into a hospital – giving the 'theatre' a whole new purpose.

A mile or so further north is another attraction which draws tourists from far and wide – the Dan-yr-Ogof caves, a complex system of underground caverns and ghettoes formed in the local limestone rocks. Some sceptics have suggested that the retention of the Welsh name – for which south Wales is not particularly noted – is because the translation – 'Under the cave Caves' – would sound a bit odd.

Ebbw Vale (Glynebwy)

Sightseers have mainly steered away from the bright lights of Ebbw Vale; the sightseers were right. This is another of the south Wales heavy industry centres that has declined over the past few decades. The town and valley are perhaps most famous for being the parliamentary constituency of Aneurin Bevan, the architect of the National Health Service, which also seems to be perpetually fighting for survival.

For a brief time there was a garden festival here but it shut down because the town could not cope with the influx of the three tourists who came.

The Gower Peninsula (Penrhyn Gŵyr)

As most tourist guides will tell you, the Gower Peninsula is one of the best unspoilt areas in Wales. Its natural beauty is not entirely enhanced by the caravan parks and souvenir shops but if you can look beyond these intrusions the views are indeed wonderful. Like Snowdonia after driving through Bethesda, Gower's appeal is strengthened by having just passed through Swansea.

One attraction that doesn't depend on the breathtaking vistas are the caves of Paviland where a human headless skeleton was unearthed in 1823. The bones, stained in red ochre, became known as the Red Lady of Paviland but later excavations proved that the lady was in fact a man who lived during the Old Stone Age which preceded the Rolling Stones period. Why a man would be stained with red dye is not known. Perhaps he belonged to a very early Freemasons' coven.

Llandaff (Llandaf)

Very close to the centre of Cardiff is a quiet spot graced by a beautiful cathedral. Llandaff (as opposed to Llandaff North) is a select suburb of the capital city with its public schools and theological college and rowing club. The village, of course, has the obligatory Chinese and Indian/Bangladeshi restaurants but fights on a Saturday night must be conducted according to the Queensbury Rules.

Just down the road the BBC has its Wales headquarters. Rather like the Vatican, this is a city within a city with its own language

('Hello darling/cariad – and that's just the commissionaire!) and its own culture (drinking on the job is not permitted unless it's part of the script or written into the employee's contract – usually a senior manager). Security here, as in every large public building in Wales, is tight – rather like some of the staff. Visitors might be frisked before being admitted. Whether you are frisked or not depends on how suspicious you look and on the particular sexual preferences of the commissionaire (see above).

Credentials for entry into the higher echelons of this august company include an undistinguished university degree, the ability to speak Welsh and a totally unfounded sense of one's own importance.

Llantrisant

The village still retains its olde worlde character even though it is only eight miles from Cardiff. This village on a hill was the home of the Victorian eccentric Dr William Price. He considered himself to be a descendant of the Druids and he went around dressed in a flowing cloak. At the age of 83 he cremated his young son and was consequently taken to court where he was acquitted of all charges.

Llantrisant was granted a charter in 1346 and still has a court 'leet' and a body of freemen who meet for a dinner every year in order to find out what a court 'leet' is. They could do worse than to dine at the curious restaurant which serves exotic fare such as buffalo, kangaroo, zebra and other delicacies. Kangaroo and chips sounds like a nice idea but be sure to order a hind leg and not a front leg, which is a bit short on the meat side.

For many years this area has been the home of the Royal Mint. This is popular with people in some of the adjacent south Wales valleys towns who are allowed in free of charge to come and see what a twenty pound note looks like.

Maesteg

If this town were known by its literal translation – 'Fair Field' – every visitor would justifiably seek compensation under the Trade Descriptions Act. Like many towns in the area, it grew (and shrivelled) in tandem with the coal industry. Many of the town's chapels, which once sprouted like mushrooms, no longer echo to the sound of hymn-singing (if you want to hear this, go to the local pub) – doors have been closed, pews have been ripped out (they're also in the pub) and organs transplanted to be replaced by boys' clubs and carpet warehouses. Yet not all is gloom. The town, we hear, is undergoing 'regeneration'. The council has evidence: a Tesco store has arrived.

Merthyr's growth to its present size began in earnest at the onset of the Industrial Revolution when large ironworks were established at Dowlais, Cyfarthfa and Penydarren to exploit the area's varied mineral wealth. But its name belongs to another age. Legend has it that a British princess, Tudful, was martyred for her Christian faith. Unkind souls now theorise that martyrdom is synonymous with stopping in the town. Its current claim to notoriety is that it is ranked as the fifth worst place to live in Britain – so it's worth going there to see for yourself.

Merthyr Tydfil/ Tudful

Monmouth/Trefynwy

Apart from its historical connections, with some events and personalities chronicled in a few of Shakespeare's plays, there is little to shout about here. You wouldn't expect much from a town that is notable only for its bridge – even though it is quite a bridge with a stone arch you have to pass through to enter and, of course, to leave the town. Leaving is much more fun.

Merthyr takes pride in its new Council offices.

69

Mumbles (Y Mwmbwls)

Different explanations exist as to how this small settlement got its name but the most compelling – at least to many people – is that French visitors – many years ago – likened it to a place across the Channel which had two protuberances resembling breasts; so Mumbles is a distortion of the French word for this part of the female anatomy. Thank goodness there wasn't a lighthouse or obelisk over the water.

Local drinkers who have attempted the famed 'Mumbles Mile' – buying and drinking a wee snort at all the watering holes situated along the rambling promenade – put forward the theory about the name that everyone who has succeeded in negotiating the alcoholic jaunt ends up mumbling incoherently.

However, the place is attractive enough for at least one eminent film star – Catherine Zeta Jones – to build a house here. In truth, the small town offers a fine assortment of decent restaurants and ice cream parlours and it 'nestles' – a fine guide book term – close to the Gower Peninsula.

A luxury home. Note the granny annex.

Neath (Castell-nedd)

This small town is one of only three places in Wales mentioned by the historian Tacitus – and this is before it established itself as a wonderful rugby town with the Welsh All-Blacks being nearly invincible at one time. Now the proud team has merged with Swansea to form a regional team called 'The Ospreys'. In 1993 a survey discovered that on the Parade in Neath was the second most likely place to encounter a fight on a Friday night. From then on, visitors have tended to come on Sundays.

Newport (Casnewydd)

This is a modest city which has much to be modest about. It is neither sleepy nor bustling. It just 'is'. Of course it has the remains of a castle but Cardiffians firmly believe that it was built not to keep enemies at bay but to keep its residents from getting out. In 1839 the town experienced the Chartist uprising. Outside the Westgate Hotel the militia fired upon a group of agitators who had marched 5,000 strong on the town. Their leader, John Frost, addressed his followers in Welsh. More recently, the denizens of Newport have had to ask themselves some puzzling questions. Are we wholly Welsh or a little bit English? Do we live in Gwent or Monmouthshire? Will our regional rugby team ever win a match?

Nearby is the Celtic Manor Resort – the grand name for a huge hotel that closely resembles the MI5 headquarters in London. It is so large that the staff are supplied with electric-powered vehicles and sat nav to find their way around. It has attracted the Ryder Cup to its golf course but since it is situated high on a hill many a stray golf ball has been picked up in the town centre.

Penarth

Now almost a suburb of Cardiff, this rather sedate town has more charity shops than places twice its size. This gives you some hint as to the general affluence of many of its inhabitants. Clothes worn more than twice are donated and bric-a-brac in the windows lures in the passer-by. The height of holiday excitement here is a walk along the pier. There is a pebble beach and sea water that rivals that of Barry Island in its engaging sepia tones.

On most beaches, it takes topless sunbathing to cause the occasional uproar. In staid and sedate Penarth the very sight of a naked female ankle is enough to keep the local paper's letters column busy for weeks.

Pontypool (Pont-y-pŵl)

For the inquisitive tourist 'bed and board' in this town would mean you were staying in a boarded-up lodging house. The decline of the town seems to have been mirrored by the dramatic misfortune of its local rugby team who slipped from national leaders to also-rans. There is a park and a small museum so allow about ten minutes for a good look around.

Pontypridd

It's a sad fact that when talking about Pontypridd, most people don't associate it with the area's industrial hey-day; they don't even link it with the old single-span bridge over the river Taff which gave the town its name. No. Pontypridd is the birthplace of Tommy Woodward, aka Tom Jones, who apparently stuck a miner's helmet down the front of his trousers, wiggled his hips and embarked on a singing career beginning with a song called 'It's not unusual'. The town heralds the start of the Rhondda Valley and deserves the cliché 'bustling'. It's a down-to-earth town where pies and pasties are favoured more than prawns and caviar.

An itinerant street-preacher

Porthcawl

This resort – the nearest thing to a Welsh equivalent of Blackpool – gained popularity when thousands of miners from the surrounding valleys thronged there to wash those little parts that a tin bath in front of the fire couldn't reach. There is a fun fair with the usual rides and stalls such as the coconut shy where punters unwittingly attempt to knock off a well-glued coconut with a wonky ball; the metal grip that descends on objects but never quite manages to grasp one for the eager customer; and the hoop-la stall where hapless merry-makers can't understand why the small wooden ring refuses to encompass gifts that are wider than the missile. In the winter, many stall-holders return to their villas in the south of France.

Port Talbot (Aberafan)

Port Talbot is notable for two things: the steelworks and the number of now famous people who lived in or near the town. Two among many are Sir Anthony Hopkins and Richard Burton. The steelworks have something of a strange beauty about them but when driving past them on the M4 with your mother-in-law sitting in the back, think twice before complaining about her total lack of control in the bowel department. It's more likely to be the ever-present smell of sulphur from the steel works.

Raglan (Rhaglan)

Another of those numerous Welsh towns which owe their fame to their castles – this one was the last to hold out against Parliament in the first Civil War. Raglan lies in the vast emptiness between Monmouth and Pontypool. Two kings of England are reputed to have spent some time at the castle – though this is no recommendation. Charles I was a guest after his defeat at the battle of Naseby, and Henry VII, before acceding to the throne, was held prisoner there. It might take the offer of a cell to persuade you to stay there too. Its other claim to fame is that the castle was not built by Edward I but by those well-known local builders ap Thomas and Herbert.

Rhondda Valleys (Y Rhondda)

The two valleys of the Rhondda Fawr and Rhondda Fach were the very heart of the South Wales Coalfields and the number of towns bear witness to the thousands who moved into the area in search of employment – Treherbert, Treorci, Tonypandy, Porth, Tylorstown, Ferndale and Maerdy, to name but a few. The economic desolation caused by pit closures in the 1980s has had little noticeable impact on the character of the locals who remain doggedly proud of their heritage.

Green creeps over the hills now instead of coal dust but politics remains fixed in the culture – even to the extent of allowing Conservative Clubs to operate. Drinks are cheaper inside and where better to enjoy a pint when bought for you by the inevitably-doomed Tory candidate.

Swansea (Abertawe)

The city's association with the world-renowned poet Dylan Thomas – he drank there, as well as here and everywhere – has attracted many tourists. Scholars have suggested that the setting for his radio play

74

The scene that inspired 'How Green was my Val

Under Milk Wood. Llareggub is a fair description of the extent of Swansea's attractions since backwards it spells 'Buggerall'. But since Dylan left, a new activity has taken root which catches the eye of any driver trying to enter or leave the city. This is the daily digging up of the main road. Since the local planners (the word is used very loosely) decided that the only main road into and out of the city would have alongside it all the major buildings, visitors can enjoy the impressive prison building, the refurbished leisure centre and Council headquarters as they spend 45 minutes crawling along the mile from Mumbles to the city centre.

Recently, the obligatory marina has blessed Swansea with a well-named Maritime Quarter – since only a quarter of the buildings seem to be fully occupied. If this represents the high life, the low life makes its presence known at weekends as the nightclubs swarm with bimbos wearing war paint and little else and tattooed Neanderthals look for a female to drag home by the hair to their sparsely-furnished cave. This savage tribe is called the Swansea Jacks.

Tintern (Tyndyrn)

The ruined abbey in this rural spot was immortalised by the poet William Wordsworth as he and his sister paused on their journey to the nearest Chinese take-away. Amid the ruins of this former Cistercian House, the visitor is left to speculate about the Spartan simplicity of the devoted monks or conjecture as to how many semis the sensitive developer could erect on a nicely levelled site.

The Vale of Glamorgan (Bro Morgannwg)

These acres of idyllic villages and pastures were once a centre of Welsh culture. It was here that the Welsh language flourished in verse and prose. Today, the 'des reses' are likely to be occupied by the odd politician and TV 'personality'. The very names of villages and hamlets – Peterston-super-Ely, St George's, Bonvilston, St Nicholas – indicate the Anglicisation of the area. To live in the Vale is, indeed, to have 'arrived'. What a blessing that many people in Wales don't even want to start the journey.

And finally...

Try something different!

Unusual sports

Just as Scotland has its Highland games, so Wales is developing its own equivalent but with a distinctly Cymric (Welsh) flavour. Inspired by new sporting facilities developed in Cardiff and Swansea, other more rural areas of Wales are attracting hosts of eager onlookers and participants.

Instead of tossing the caber, athletes are training to toss the *crempog* (pancake). It's not as heavy as a large tree trunk but the frying pans are quite a weight. At the mediaeval village (reconstructed) at Cosmeston, near Penarth, a variant on the jousting tournament now takes place. Dressed in full armour, the contestants gallop towards each other on large sheep and, having each consumed a minimum of eight leeks and twelve spring onions, they blow breath through each other's visors and the one who recoils off his steed because of the stink is declared the sad loser.

In parts of Powys, sheepdog trials have been replaced by an annual event called 'herding the peasants'. Titled landowners – many from England – have trained Rottweilers to respond to whistles. The aim is to round up a large group of farm workers and direct them through fields and into a large pond. The sport is very humane as each peasant is equipped with wellies and a wet suit. Last century this event replaced the former peasant shoot although in some parts of Wales pheasants are let loose instead.

In west Wales a local form of badminton is played using shuttle cockles while in North Wales a local adaptation of bear-baiting is a popular sport which takes place in secret locations. An unpopular councillor is tied to a stake and insults are hurled at him or her until they can take no more and promise to resign.

We must mention one other uniquely Welsh and particularly challenging sport that flourished during the Seventies and Eighties, i.e. holiday home burning. The competitor's task was to burn a house down without the knowledge of the local police, CID and MI5 yet with the full knowledge and approval of the local population. Visitors to twenty first century Wales may be relieved to know that this sport is now extinct.

Getting around

Leave your car behind and enjoy the excitement of travelling around Wales in more exhilarating forms of transport.

Take an open-top bus

to go sightseeing in Cardiff. There's not much point sitting downstairs but at least you'll be safe from pigeon droppings. Also in Cardiff, you can enjoy being pedalled around in a modern-day **rickshaw**. It's just like being in China except they don't shoot you in Cardiff if you happen to go through a red light.

Why not hire a **bicycle** and visit parts of scenic Wales that you could never get access to by car – like forests and municipal car parks. Ask

77

a complete stranger if they'll share a tandem with you and have a bet on who falls off first. Go **pony trekking** but show who's boss. One tourist who was a bit apprehensive about being on horse-back gave in to a wilful nag. The result was that, having mounted the animal in Aberystwyth for a morning's jaunt to Aberaeron, the hapless rider ended up in Rhyl and had to return the horse by packing it onto a train – with the assistance of four guards, three police officers and a crane.

Look out for helpful teenagers if you are in a large city or town. They will lend you their **skateboard** in return for a long-term loan of your mobile phone and credit cards. If they don't own a skateboard, they will be only too pleased to get you a shopping trolley. Take an **aeroplane** to get you from north to south of the country and back again or walk to the top of Snowdon and see if you can **hang-glide** onto the heliport in Cardiff.

Of course you can always take a **boat** to visit one of several bird sanctuaries off the coasts of Wales, such as Flat Holm, Skokholm or Skomer. But much more adventurous would be to hop into a **canal barge** and enjoy a restful cruise. The advantage of taking this form of transport is that, in the wet season in Wales – that's from January to December – you can easily glide off the canal and down the main street of a nearby town and do your shopping.

By whatever form of transport you travel you will be welcome to return as a valued visitor.

Croeso i Gymru. Welcome to Wales.

A brief history of Wales

Many people who use this guide probably know very little about the history of Wales. In fact, most Welsh people know little about their country's history. So here's a chance to put that right. Here we present some historical and hysterical facts about Cymru.

Let us start with a condensed version of how Wales evolved through many hundreds of years.

2500 BC Nice cave you've got there.

Yeah, Not bad. It's a Bronze Age semi. Could do with a door but you can't have everything.

1200 Who are all these immigrants coming in? What are they called? Celts?

100 BC Can't understand a word they're saying. It's all Greek to me.

50 AD Druids v Romans. It's an away win.

74 AD Wales 1 Romans 1 . A creditable draw.

400 AD Ta ta Romans. You tried your best. Thanks for the roads and you've left us some cracking tourist attractions.

450 – The Dark Ages. Who nicked all the candles?

600 AD They've all gone to the churches.

Oh not another invasion, Who is it this time? The who?

The Anglo what? – Saxons? Have they got planning permission for that? What's it called?

Offa's Dyke. To separate us from England? That's an 'offa' we can't refuse!

800 AD What's the matter with people? It's the bleeding Vikings now. Get a life. Leave us alone.

1066 AD Thought it was too good to last. Now it's those nutters from France. Norman somebody or other. Well, at least they're having a go at the English as well. Carry on Norman.

1100 AD Hang on. Now it's a few kings of England throwing their weight around.

1200 AD Hail Llewellyn – a true Prince of Wales. He'll show those English.

That's not fair. There's more of them than us.

1300s Nice castles. Shame about the tenants.

1400s Another true Prince of Wales – Owain Glyndŵr. Henry VII crowned.

He's one of us. Pity about his son. The Act of Union? You must be joking. It won't last.

1500 – At last – we can now read the Bible in Welsh

1700s Hurray! The Welsh language is on the march.

1800s It took us a while but now it's not about bronze – it's all about coal, iron and steel

early 1900s We're getting organised. Throw your Dai caps in the air. We've got unions. No, not onions – unions. The chapels are thriving – hide your beer!

Liberals in. Liberals out. Labour in. Labour still in. Hang on.

The bombing school on the Llŷn Peninsula has spontaneously combusted. What a shame.

1950s Radical Welsh-speaking movements come to the fore. The Free Wales Army causes a stir. Not bad for three blokes and a dog.

Was the dog Welsh-speaking?

He wouldn't say.

2000 – Wales now has a sort of Parliament – the Welsh Assembly.

Today What's happening? Even the Tories are pretending to be Welsh.

It's a revolution. Well – devolution. So what's next? Self-government? So soon? It's only taken us 3,000 years. Steady on.

Some Magical Moments in Wales

You've probably heard of Merlin the Welsh Wizard. Well, he's still working his magic in Wales. In fact, he never stopped waving his wand. How else can you explain the following amazing phenomena?

Cardiff City win the FA Cup in 1927

The only football team ever to take the Cup out of England. It was against the mighty Arsenal. The game looked like heading for extra time when that cunning little Scot, Hughie Ferguson, shot at goal. It was not by any means a blistering shot but somehow – the goalkeeper, Dan Lewis managed to lie over the ball which squirmed under his prostrate body and into the net.

Now our Dan was a Welshman and who else but Merlin would have had him selected against a Welsh club and who else but the Welsh Wizard would have created a small hole for the ball to creep into and under the goalie's body? And who else but Merlin would have arranged for the match to be played on April 23rd – St George's Day, with the Welsh Prime Minister David Lloyd George in attendance. He didn't manage to arrange for Dan Lewis to be rewarded with the freedom of Cardiff but he probably thought that would look a bit suspicious. Merlin is nobody's fool.

Pen-y-berth Bombing School appears to spontaneously combust

The year is 1936 and three eminent Welshmen are arranging a barbecue. Plaid Cymru – the Welsh Nationalist Party – had been formed ten years earlier and the three chaps were organising a celebratory branch meeting. They looked around for a suitable site for the barbecue and found a lovely spot near what was a really impressive building except the British Government had bulldozed it down to build the RAF bombing school. Three sites had been identified in England but the locals objected to it. The locals near Pen-y-Berth had also objected but their protests were ignored. Anyway, Saunders Lewis, a university lecturer, writer and journalist was in charge of the hot dogs, D. J. Williams, former miner and schoolteacher brought the drinks (non-alcoholic) and the Rev. Lewis Valentine, a Baptist minister was organising the sausages.

Everyone was having a jolly time when the Rev. threw a few too many sausages on the barbecue and the fat ignited and flew towards the bombing School. No-one wanted to shout 'FIRE!' in case some lunatic had a gun – so the bombing school was destroyed. Now how could a bit of sausage fat burn down a whole building? Merlin knows. His long years with King Arthur had turned him into a pacifist and he didn't want to have an instrument of war in his backyard. Good old Merlin.

The strange case of political metamorphosis

Merlin has a wicked sense of humour. Once upon a time there were two well-known Welsh politicians – one from South Wales; the other from North Wales. One Welsh-speaking; the other had no Welsh except his accent. One was in the Labour Party; the other in Plaid Cymru. They had nothing in common except, in their own way, they were rather radical. Neil Kinnock, the Labour man, professed to being a communist in his student days and Dafydd Elis Thomas, the Plaid fellow, joined a splinter group within his party because they believed their political colleagues were becoming too respectable and mainstream.

Well, as time passed, Mr Kinnock became the leader of the Labour Party and became almost famous for opposing the setting up of a Welsh Assembly, falling down on a beach and getting wet and shouting a silly chant at his party conference. Oh yes – and for losing the General Election.

Meanwhile Mr Elis Thomas had also risen to great heights by becoming an MP and later the Presiding Officer once the Welsh Assembly was established (Neil lost that vote as well). Merlin looked on and thought: 'I'm going to change these two ugly ducklings into swans' (not that they were really ugly). And ABRACADABRA! they both became peers of the realm, sitting with all the hereditary nobles and occasionally turning up to wear a bit of ermine. What a transformation; from left wing radicals to a seat in the House of Lords. Others followed but they were the originals. Some uncharitable commentators now refer to them as Fraud Kinnock and Fraud Elis Thomas. Naughty Merlin!

A National Assembly comes to Wales

In 1999 Merlin waved his wand and changed an initial NO vote into a YES vote from the people of Wales. Now, all at once, we had an extra 60 politicians to support. To honour the occasion a brand new building was commissioned. The splendid City Hall in Cardiff was not good enough. The AMs (Assembly Members) wanted a spanking new multi-million pound edifice. What they (and we) got was a large pagoda stuck onto acres of glass and standing on several layers of slate. Not a tree, bush or blade of grass in sight. Well,

that would have put the price up by a couple of quid. at least. Here in this stark palace the worthy politicians pass 'measures' instead of laws, but all this may change and the Assembly could become a Parliament – literally a place where people talk – a pretty accurate description. of what goes on there.

A few AMs have gained some much-needed publicity by over-indulging in the dreaded alcohol.

It's the stress, you understand, of working sometimes up to 12 hours a week. Merlin – how could you be so heartless?

Dr Who makes his home in Cardiff

What an amazing happening! *Dr Who* – that incredibly popular sci-fi TV series uses Cardiff as its prime location. No – Merlin wasn't responsible for creating that coup. He watches very little telly. Where he comes in handy is being responsible for

all the special effects: people flying through the air; rockets going off, comedy actors trying to act dramatically. That's all Merlin that is. But there's been a hitch and Merlin will need all his powers to resolve this. Dr Who's Tardis has disappeared. No one knows for certain where it's gone but there is a rumour that a family of fourteen evicted from their Council house for having their telly on too loud while watching Dr Who are now living in the Tardis somewhere on the outskirts of the city.

Merlin hasn't managed to find it yet. So he's either losing his touch, has lost his wand or feels sorry for the family of fourteen for the special effects can be very noisy indeed.

And now for some...

Misconceptions about Wales

1. Welsh men find sheep physically attractive

This is not true. Welsh men do not find sheep attractive nor do sheep find Welsh men attractive, as far as we can tell. Just because there are more sheep in Wales than there are women doesn't mean anything. There are no doubt more birds, ants and woodlice as well. No – this myth was propagated by a particularly thick non-Celtic yobbo who heard about a sheep-shearing contest and thought it was some kind of sexual Olympics.

2. Welsh people live in caves

We stopped doing that several thousand years ago. Now we live in accommodation quite similar to the dwellings of people across the Severn Bridge – except for a small semi-Neanderthal tribe of inhabitants in the west of England who live in caves near to Cheddar and who eat nothing but cheese.

3. All Welsh people can sing

This is not entirely true. The last census discovered a few men living on an offshore island near the coast of Wales who can not sing. Or more accurately who don't sing. That's because they are all Trappist monks. Considering the fact that they produce wine and spirits with a very high alcohol content it's not surprising that they can't talk – let alone sing.

4. The Welsh are good at rugby

It's true that the Welsh Rugby team occasionally win the Six Nations Championship and the Grand Slam but the team soon remembers that historically they have always been underdogs and therefore should not be so presumptuous as to keep on winning. That's why, after a good season, we then go on to lose the next 25 games on the trot. The trouble is our players are not hard. Valleys women on a night out clubbing in the middle of winter and wearing only a dish cloth – now they're hard, really hard. They should form the Welsh team. It's worth a try – or two!

5. Dylan Thomas is a poetic hero in Wales

No getting away from it; he was a talented individual but after *Under Milk Wood* and one well-known poem, on what does his reputation stand? True, he could down the odd pint and he got out of his head on whisky. But he didn't just get drunk on whisky; he got drunk on his own verbosity. In other words, he suffered from chronic verbal diarrhoea. And dear old Dylan was the bloke who said:'Land of my Fathers? My fathers can keep it!'. Perhaps we should forgive him for saying that. He was probably under the influence of his own ego.

Some unsung and unknown Welsh heroes and heroines

Forget your well-known celebrities and politicians. They get enough publicity. Recent historical research has brought to light some marvellous men and women who shaped the very fabric of Welsh society: its history and its culture. Let us begin with…

The man who dug the Glamorganshire Canal all on his own

One day, in 1793, Dic 'The Dig' Davies started digging a trench to plant some potatoes on his smallholding near Merthyr Tydfil in South Wales. But as fast as he could dig, the ditch filled up with water. But Dic was not one to give up so he kept digging – and the water kept filling the trench. His wife was getting worried. Where was Dic? And then someone told her they had seen Dic half way to Cardiff still digging on what was common land because he didn't want to be jailed for trespassing. Soon Dic had forgotten why he had started digging in the first place. He was now being egged on by crowds who had gathered to see this human mole. 'Why are you digging butt?' they cried and Dic would shout back: 'It's good exercise'.

It was months before Dic could see Cardiff Castle looming in the distance. He had dug his way from Merthyr to Cardiff and received a hero's welcome and a civic reception when he arrived. It was not long before an entrepreneur saw the potential for creating a canal to ship the iron and coal from Merthyr to the port of Cardiff. So Dic's potato trench was widened and in 1794 the Glamorganshire Canal was officially opened by Dic and his long-suffering wife. And as a special award Dic was presented with a full bag of potatoes by the Lord Mayor of Cardiff. What an amazing story. It's hard to believe it could have happened!

The woman who created the traditional Welsh hat

Hannah Hughes from Llandeilo in mid Wales was a law-abiding working class woman who had nine children. Her husband couldn't work because he had chronic catarrh. So it was difficult for Hannah to make ends meet. There was no welfare system in the early nineteenth century. One or two of her children worked down the coal mines but their pay was pathetically small.

One day, in the winter, with the snow falling heavily, Hannah looked in her coal scuttle and it was empty. She was desperate to heat their small parlour. How could she get wood and coal? She could gather wood legally from the woods nearby but coal gave off much more heat. So Hannnah thought the unthinkable. She would have to steal what she could from the small heaps of coal lying about a mile away. But how to conceal it? Then she had a brilliant idea. What if she could hide the coal under a hat – a black hat. There was no point wearing her usual little Sunday best hat so she set about making a very tall hat which would accommodate a fair amount of coal. And so she did. She made what later caught on as the traditional Welsh hat now pictured in a famous paiting where a lady is wearing the tall cone-shaped hat as she enters the chapel. Nowadays Hannah could have worn a traffic cone on her head and painted it black. But that's another story.

The man who invented the Welsh emblem: the leek

Owain Glyndŵr, the famous Welsh warrior, called on his trusty blacksmith Hywel the Hammer. 'In three days' time' he said, 'we shall be marching against the English invaders. I want something on the front of our shields that will shoot fear through their veins' (Owain was very poetic). 'Devise for me a prototype (He was also very literate) by this evening and bring it to my tent'. 'Done!' shouted Hywel and off he went. He toiled all day with his blacksmith's tools fashioning a fearful sign. That evening he took his creation to

Owain's tent and proudly displayed what he had done. 'What in the name of all that's holy is THAT?' bellowed Owain. 'It's a common leek but shaped like a phallic symbol to frighten the enemy into realising that we Welsh are real men'. 'It certainly frightens me' said his leader. 'Can you hammer out the odd 2000 overnight?' 'Done!' said Hywel the hammer (He wasn't very literate).

And so the humble leek became a Welsh emblem. A dragon might have been a little bit more scary but at least he didn't produce a daffodil.

The gamekeeper who bred the first Welsh corgi

Everyone knows that the Royal Family have kept corgis for many decades and they do indeed have a royal connection that goes back many centuries. It all began when a Welsh farmer and rich landowner was fed up with his gamekeeper's inability to bring home his cattle in time for milking as punctually as the rich landowner would wish. So he told the gamekeeper whose name was Bryn (meaning 'hill' – but that's irrelevant) that he was a bit slow with the cattle because he was now 95 and getting a bit long in the tooth and short in the breath. So he instructed Bryn to buy a dog that could round up the cattle and steer them towards the cowsheds.

Well, Bryn tried many types of dogs but not one of them was good enough. The cattle just kicked them away. So Bryn realised he needed a dog with little legs to bite the ankles of the cows – and the occasional bull – to bully them (sorry) homewards. Bryn then borrowed a Labrador from a nearby farm and crossed it with a weasel that he had caught in one of the barns. The Labrador was quite happy but the weasel was a bit put out. Anyway, the trial was successful and the very first corgi was born. Very soon the news reached the Royal Family's King George III who was being troubled with poachers on some of his estates. So he ordered a brace of corgis to snap at the heels of those peasants and round them up to face the full force of the law. And from then on corgis have been a real royal favourite.

The first woman to make a Welsh rarebit

This is perhaps the most amazing historical fact of them all. In the nineteenth century people who committed all types of crimes were transported to Van Diemen's Land which is now known as Tasmania. Some lawbreakers, such as our heroine Glenys Pritchard, were sent away for what we would consider to be really petty misdemeanours. She poached a rabbit. No, she didn't cook it (she did later of course as we shall find out). She stole it. So Glenys was sent off to Tasmania where she served ten years of hard labour.

When she returned to her little Welsh village she had acquired two things: one was a hatred of rabbits; the other was an unmistakeable Aussie accent. Then, one day, she looked out of her window and saw a horse and cart jolt as it passed by. Out of curiosity Glenys went outside and saw what was an early example of road kill. The carriage had squashed a rabbit. Glenys was delighted. At last she could get her own back in a strange sort of way. So she didn't need to prepare the rabbit. It was squashed so flat you could hardly tell what it was. She cooked the flat rabbit and invited her neighbour in to share the meal. 'What's that?' asked the neighbour as she looked at what could have been a piece of cheese for all she could tell. 'It's a Welsh rabbit' replied Glenys in her Aussie accent. 'A Welsh rarebit?' said the neighbour and after she had told some of her friends what she had eaten the rare delicacy had been officially named.

The Rebecca Riots: A Dramatisation

In the western part of Wales in the late 1830s some Welsh farmers were becoming more and more annoyed about their treatment by the powers that be. The last straw was the erection of toll-gates, the revenue being intended to finance the building of new roads. A posse of men dressed in women's clothes and with blackened faces rode on horseback (possibly side-saddle) and tore down the gates. This recently discovered fragment of a contemporary drama about the events catches the moment of decision making and the finale clearly shows the spirited commitment of those Welsh rebels.

Dic *Well I'm sick of paying. I haven't got two groats to rub together.*

Mic *Well I keep my groats separate.*

Ric *So what are we gonna do about it boys?*

Vic *Smash the tolls. Break down the gates.*

Dic *Yes – smash them. Chop them down.*

Mic *No more paying.*

Ric *Break the gates.*

Vic *Now then boys – listen. All this talk is not going to change things. We've got to act.*

Mic *That's right. We've got to act and act now.*

Ric *To be or not to be – that is the question.*

Vic *What are you doing?*

Ric *He said we've got to act.*

Mic *No – I meant DO something.*

Dic *We'll smash the gates down.*

Mic *What with?*

Ric *Well I've got a chopper.*

Vic *We can do it late at night.*

Dic *Aye – and we can do it in disguise so we don't get caught.*

Mic *We'll smash the gates.*

Ric *And we'll all have big…*

Vic *Yes, we all know.*

Dic *I'll use my bare hands.*

Mic *Wear gloves though.*

Dic *Why?*

Mic *Well, to disguise them.*

Ric *Yes – we can do it in disguise.*

Dic *I've got a mask.*

Vic *With a face like yours I'm not surprised.*

Mic *We could wear hoods.*

Ric *No, hoodies have got a bad name.*

Vic *I know ! I know! I know!*

All 3 *Yes! Yes! Yes!*

Vic *We can all dress as women.*

SILENCE

Dic *Well I'm not sure about that. Where am I gonna get a dress from?*

Mic *I can lend you one of mine PAUSE Well it's a smock really.*

Dic *A frock?*

Mic *No – a smock.*

AND SO THE PLOT WAS HATCHED. THEY WOULD ALL DRESS AS WOMEN – AN EVENT KNOWN HISTORICALLY AS THE TRANSVESTITURE.

THEN THE FIRST NIGHT OF ACTION…

Ric *Do I look like a woman?*

Vic *Well you walk like one.*

Mic *Does my bum look big in this?*

Dic *Big! I thought I was looking at the horse.*

Vic *Right. We all need to look and act like women.*

Mic *Yes, we must go down…*

Vic *Pardon?*

HA! HA! HA! HA!

WHAT'S SO FUNNY, MATE?

Mic ...in history.

Vic Oh!

Dic Now to go down in history we need a fancy female name.

Mic What about the Pussycat Dolls?

Ric No you idiot, this is Carmarthenshire 1839.

Mic Ok. Just trying to help.

Vic Now – it has to be something dramatic – something... biblical.

Dic Look – open the bible – there – Rebecca. That's it. The Rebecca Riots.

Mic Right. Are we all ready?

Ric Yeah – let's go. Smash those booths and tolls down.

Vic We may be men but don't forget – tonight we are all WOMEN.

Dic Women? Oh yes, that's a problem. The two of us can't go then.

Vic What? Why not?

Dic Well he's washing his hair and I've got a headache.

Wacky Wales is just one of a huge range of entertaining and informative books about Wales published by Y Lolfa. For a full list of books currently in print, go now to our website where you can browse and order on-line. We also supply paper catalogues free of charge upon request.

Talybont Ceredigion Cymru/Wales SY24 5HE
www.ylolfa.com
ylolfa@ylolfa.com
01970 832 304